W9-DAX-075

Secrets
of
Selling
Services

Humber College Library
3199 Lakeshore Blvd. West
Toronto, ON   M8V 1K8

Secrets

— of —

Selling

Services

Everything You Need to Sell What Your Customer Can't See—from Pitch to Close

Stephan Schiffman

New York Chicago San Francisco Lisbon London Madrid Mexico City
Milan New Delhi San Juan Seoul Singapore Sydney Toronto

HUMBER LIBRARIES LAKESHORE CAMPUS
3199 Lakeshore Blvd West
TORONTO, ON.   M8V 1K8

DISCARD

The *McGraw-Hill* Companies

Copyright © 2013 by Stephan Schiffman. All rights reserved. Printed in the United States of America. Except as permitted under the United States Copyright Act of 1976, no part of this publication may be reproduced or distributed in any form or by any means, or stored in a data base or retrieval system, without the prior written permission of the publisher.

1 2 3 4 5 6 7 8 9 0   QFR/QFR   1 8 7 6 5 4 3 2

ISBN   978-0-07-179162-5
MHID   0-07-179162-0

e-ISBN   978-0-07-179163-2
e-MHID   0-07-179163-9

McGraw-Hill books are available at special quantity discounts to use as premiums and sales promotions or for use in corporate training programs. To contact a representative, please e-mail us at bulksales@mcgraw-hill.com.

This book is printed on acid-free paper.

To Julia Anne Heffernan,
and to her brother, mother, and father

CONTENTS

ACKNOWLEDGMENTS

My sincere thanks for the success of this project go to Monika Verma, Gary Krebs, Donya Dickerson, Tom Jared, Darren Newton, Anthony Bartolo, Tobias W. Heffernan, Joshua Michael Sanders, and, of course, Anne, Daniele, and Jennifer.

Equally significant are all those salespeople who go out each day to prospect, meet new people, and make sales. These are my true inspiration. Thank you, all.

INTRODUCTION

It was an odd situation.

In fact, I couldn't remember when I'd last run into the problem. During four decades of selling, I've encountered almost every conceivable reaction, from clients who acted as if I'd brought them Aladdin's magic lamp to others who clearly couldn't wait to show me the door. Emotionally, they'd run the gamut from eager enthusiasm to the sort of gloom-and-doom pessimism that would make Eeyore seem in comparison like a cheerleader for the Dallas Cowboys.

But in all those years, the clients had understood what I was selling. I didn't think it was particularly complicated. Yet here was this pleasant young man, dressed in a neat suit and tie and sitting behind an orderly desk, staring at me as if I'd asked him to explain Einstein's Theory of the Unified Field. His brows were drawn together, and he tapped a pencil nervously on the pad in front of him. I noticed, with trepidation, that he'd yet to take a single note. Not a good sign.

He shook his head. "I'm sorry, Steve, but I still don't get it. Just what is it that your company is offering to do for us?"

I suppressed a sigh, straightened my tie, and tried to keep my voice light and genial. "We're sales trainers. We train people how to sell. And I can come into your company, make a presentation to your sales force, and work with your salespeople. In the end, you'll find that as a result of my training, you'll see a substantial uptick in your sales."

He still looked puzzled. "So you're selling me a package of CDs with sales presentations?"

"Uh, no." I tried again. "I'd actually come to your company in person and do presentations."

"But why wouldn't I want my own sales director to do that?" he asked. It wasn't a smart-ass question or a way of pushing back against my presentation. He genuinely wanted to know.

"Well," I countered, "he could, of course. But what I'm offering is a long record of experience in selling and half a million salespeople trained."

He shook his head. "That sounds very impressive, Steve, but I don't know how to measure that. I don't know how to put a specific dollar value on what you're offering, and that makes me very nervous." He smiled faintly. "And I never like being nervous."

Much later, when the call had come to an uneasy conclusion (we agreed to meet in two weeks after he'd had time to study the materials I left with him and discuss the matter with his sales director and CFO), and I was heading back to the office, I turned the matter over and over in my mind. Some salespeople can push a bad or mediocre sales call out of their minds immediately, but I'm not one of them. I kept wondering if there was something I could have said or done that might have made things go in a different direction. Was there a fundamental problem with my presentation? I was pretty sure there wasn't, because this was the same basic presentation I'd been making, with a considerable degree of success, for a lot of years, and I didn't think the world had suddenly changed in the past 24 hours.

So what was the difficulty?

It finally came to me—and it's probably come to you already. What he didn't get was that I wasn't selling a thing, an object, a physical product. Instead, I was selling a service, something that by its nature is intangible. And for many people, this is something that's harder to grasp.

As it happens, I had an opportunity to test my theory a week or two later. I was attending a wedding out of town, one at which I didn't know most of the people. After watching the bride go down the aisle and applauding when the minister presented the newly married couple to the assembled guests, we broke for a short cocktail hour before the dinner. I had an opportunity to chat with some of my fellow guests and get to know them a bit. However, I carefully refrained from saying what I did for a living. Bearing in mind my experience of some weeks earlier, I saw this as a chance to find out more about the distinction people make between selling a service and selling a product.

When we sat down for dinner, I was with a table of people I didn't know other than a few minutes of casual talk over drinks. We bantered back and forth, mostly about the now-married couple and how lovely the ceremony had been. Finally, someone looked at me and said, "So, Steve, what do you do for a living?"

I replied, "I sell sales training."

There was a brief silence. I looked carefully at the faces of my fellow guests. On one or two I could see an expression that said, clearly, "Yikes! A salesperson. Better not talk to him, or he'll want us to buy a car or something." (This is a common reaction when I tell people I'm in sales.) The other people were split. About half of them were nodding as if to say, "Yeah, okay, interesting." The other half were looking completely puzzled. One of them broke the silence with almost exactly the same question that had been posed by the CEO a couple of weeks before: "What's that mean, exactly?"

Keeping this experience in mind, a few days later when I was presenting to a group of salespeople, I told them, "I sell the service of sales training. What do you think that means?"

Hands immediately shot up in the air. Virtually everyone in the room got it right away and gave me a long, thorough answer. But it proved to me that even though salespeople know what selling a service means, other people don't. And those are the people we're selling to.

That's why I decided to write this book. It's clear that too often we're not doing a good job of explaining the distinction between an object that people can see and touch and evaluate with their eyes and hands—and, more important, one that it's apparently easy to put a dollar value on—and something that's more abstract, whether it's accounting, legal advice, HR training, or, in my case, sales training.

It's equally clear to me, after talking to a lot of salespeople in the field, that they have a harder time selling services than products. They aren't sure what to say, they don't know how to quantify what they're offering, and they generally have a harder time showing the client the specific benefits of the service. This is especially true when the service is something the client already has and the salesperson is trying to sell an upgrade of the service. I'll explain the reasons for this difficulty later in the book.

The good news is that I think there is a simple truth at the heart of this problem, and once we master it, selling service becomes easier. The truth is this: *Service is a product.* It's true that it's a different kind of a product, but it's a product, nonetheless. This is at the heart of the difficulty, and it's a difficulty that we and the clients have created for ourselves. So the main challenge we face as salespeople is to erase the artificial distinction that has grown up between services and products and get clients to realize that both of them do the same essential thing: they solve a problem.

With that in mind, let's get down to it.

SELLING WHAT YOU CAN'T SEE

In Arthur Conan Doyle's immortal Sherlock Holmes story "The Adventure of Silver Blaze," there occurs the following dialogue between Holmes and the none-too-bright local inspector of police who has been called in to solve the crime of a kidnapped racehorse.

The inspector says, "Is there any other point to which you would wish to draw my attention?"

Holmes responds, "To the curious incident of the dog in the nighttime."

"The dog did nothing in the nighttime."

"That was the curious incident," remarked Sherlock Holmes.

It's one of the most famous exchanges in the whole Sherlock Holmes canon, and one that's stayed with me since I read it more than 50 years ago. It's like trying to put your foot onto a stair and realizing the stair isn't there. It disconcerts you at first because Holmes is calling your attention to something that *didn't* happen rather than something that *did*.

In a way, that's what selling a service can feel like. When you sell a physical product—say, computers—you're selling a product that can be described in terms of its physical attributes. The computer you're selling has so much memory, this many bytes of capacity, comes with this number of preinstalled programs, and so on. Furthermore, you can describe it very specifically in terms that anyone, including those who aren't computer geniuses, can understand: it's so many inches wide by so many inches tall, weighs thus and such many pounds, has a screen of so many inches in dimension, and so on.

In Holmesian terms, it's the thing that *did* happen, the object we can see, pick up, punch buttons on, and so forth.

But when you're selling service contracts for computers, what you're selling is a promise to fix a problem that hasn't happened yet. You're selling on the potential of your solution, something the client has a harder time envisioning.

In other words, you're asking the client to look at something that hasn't happened—a dog in the nighttime, so to speak.

As it happens, I experienced an illustration of this point a day or two before starting work on this chapter. I'd bought my wife a DVD player—something she could take on train or plane trips to watch movies or television shows. I'd given it to her as a Christmas present the previous year. Several weeks ago, it started to develop some hiccups. Finally, it pretty much stopped working, so I took it into the store from which I'd bought it.

"Do you have a service contract on this?" was the first question out of the mouth of the teenage salesperson at the customer service desk. (Why is it that the people who work in computer stores keep getting younger? I know it can't be because I'm getting older.)

Now, for the life of me I couldn't remember if I'd purchased a service contract. The kid looked it up on the computer for me, after giving me a look that said plainly that I must be doddering on the edge of senility. As it turned out, I'd bought a two-year service contract, so the repair on the player was free. I was struck by my foresight, but also by the fact that the person who'd originally sold

me the DVD player had been convincing enough that I'd anticipated that something might go wrong with it in two years.

Service contracts, of course, can be a bit of a gamble. If nothing goes wrong with the appliance on which you've taken out the
contract, you feel as if you've wasted your money—and, in one
sense, you have. On the other hand, if the appliance breaks it's very
nice to call up the company and tell them they're going to have to
make the repairs for free. Selling something like a service contract
requires you to make the customer aware of possibilities, most of
which he doesn't really want to contemplate.

Insurance is another type of service contract that needs this
kind of salesmanship. It's all about discussing various possible events
with your client, none of which are going to be good for her or
him. Who wants to sit down with a client and say, "So, let's talk
about what happens when you're dismembered in a car crash"?
It's this sort of thing that makes selling insurance such a challenge.

But selling other types of services can be equally difficult.
For instance, let's imagine you're selling an accounting service
to a growing company. The company representative may, quite
reasonably, remark that they already have an accountant, so they
don't need your more comprehensive service. What you've got
to convince her of is that what you're selling will improve the
kind of accounting she's getting, even though she can't see the
results right in front of her. It will allow her to grow her company
while expanding her accounting practices to meet increasingly
complex challenges.

On the other hand, you might say that if she doesn't purchase
your accounting service, she'll see negative results. As her company
grows, the challenge of having just one in-house accountant will at
some point become unsustainable. Inevitably, errors and problems
will creep into her accounting and affect all parts of her business.
Of course, none of this is happening right now, but you can predict
that it will happen in the future.

In other words, you're drawing her attention to a possibility, an intangible. You're selling the dog that did nothing in the night-time.

SELLING A PROMISE

Something they can't see always seems much more difficult to get people to grasp than what they *can* see. It's not merely a matter of the sense experience, it's a question of getting them to think in abstract terms. For instance, it's relatively easy to describe an umbrella as long as you're thinking of it merely in specific terms. An umbrella is an object. It's about four feet long, in my case, black, and is made of a combination of plastic, nylon, and metal. Ask someone to tell you what an umbrella looks like, and chances are you'll get a pretty good description.

However, the minute you turn to the more complex problem of what an umbrella is used for, you enter a more complicated world. An umbrella, most obviously, can keep the rain off you. It can also keep off the sun, it can provide a privacy shield if you're walking in public, and—if you've ever read the Winnie the Pooh stories, as I did when I was young—it can be a boat during a flood. In other words, an umbrella is a series of possibilities.

In the same way, when you're selling a service, you're selling possibilities. You're selling something that hasn't yet happened but that you want the client to place a value on. You're asking the client to think not of what she can see or touch or value immediately but of something that's a promise from you to her.

Let's take the instance of legal services. These are often something that a business doesn't need immediately but on a case-by-case basis. It's true that you'll need someone to review your contracts and guide you through the complex thicket of federal and state regulations. But the real time legal representation comes in handy is when you encounter a lawsuit or some other kind of legal action. In that case, you want your lawyer to swing into action with no ifs, and, or buts. As playwright George S. Kaufman once remarked, "The kind of lawyer I want is one who, when he's not talking to me, is home studying law."

However, when you engage a legal firm to represent you on a permanent basis, chances are you're not faced with these conditions. You're hiring a service from the lawyers, based on their promise that when you need them, they'll be there.

We'll talk much more about this concept as we get into this book. But for right now, let's focus on this basic idea: *A service is a promise*. It's a promise that when you're needed, you'll do what's wanted.

SELLING TRUST

This leads to a second concept that's essential to selling services. The most important thing you're selling to the client is your integrity. A promise isn't worth much of anything unless the client believes you'll deliver. So you've got to convince her or him that no matter what the circumstances, you'll be there. You're reliable and incorruptible. If you say you'll be in court on a certain date, you'll be there. If you promise a reliable, accurate accounting of the client's books, that's what you'll deliver. If you guarantee to keep your client's computers up and running 24-7, then that's what she or he can expect.

I have a theory about this that is based on restaurants. No, wait. Really.

I don't go out to eat at restaurants all that often, in the normal course of things. But since I'm away from home a lot, traveling, I've gotten used to dining out. And I've eaten in all levels of dining establishments. This has included everything from four-star restaurants in Manhattan to a greasy spoon diner in a small town in South Dakota. (Interestingly, the food in the greasy spoon was better than some four-star restaurants—at least I thought so at the time I ate it. But it may just have been the ambiance.)

When I go into a top restaurant in New York or Boston or Chicago or San Francisco, I generally expect a certain level of service:

- I expect that when I sit down, my server will show up in a matter of a minute or so.

- I expect that water will be on the table without me having to ask for it.

- I expect my drink order will be taken within three or four minutes of sitting down.

- I expect the waiter will check back with me after the meal has been served and will continue to check back at intervals of about 10 to 15 minutes.

- I expect to be asked whether I want to see a dessert menu.

I expect all these things because that's what I'm paying for. When I receive the bill at the end of the evening, it's not just for the quality of the food (though, of course, that's part of it), it's for the level of service provided. And I'm paying a significant price in order not to worry about those things.

In the same way, a client who pays for top-of-the-line legal service is paying, in part, for a comfort level. She's forking over a huge amount of money so that she doesn't have to worry whether her lawyer is going to know what to say to whom in court and is going to have the latest case law at his fingertips.

From all of this, we can take away one of the fundamental truths of selling what people can't see: What you're really selling is trust. You need to make the client trust you. And that doesn't change, whether it's selling legal services or waiting tables.

CLIENT CHALLENGE: "WHAT CAN YOU DO FOR ME, ANYWAY?"

Let's listen in on the following exchange:

Client: I don't know why we're talking this morning. There's no way you can possibly understand what we're going through.

Salesperson: No, I've got a very clear idea. I've got more than 10 years' experience in the field, and I can tell you, I've seen just about any kind of situation you can imagine.

Client: Uh huh. Right. Well, all right. Why don't you tell me what sort of changes you'd like to see around my company?

Salesperson: Well, for a start, there's much too long a lag time between the point when product arrives in your warehouse and the time when it gets to your factory floor. It seems as if you're missing some significant efficiencies there. I'll be happy to eliminate them for you and show you how to realize an immediate 10 percent in profit. But you'll have to be willing to change some of the antiquated ways you're used to doing things.

Client: Let's just end this right here.

Oh, dear. It's hard to see what went right in this sales call. It's over almost before it started, and when we look at it objectively, it's not hard to see why the client is angry.

LET THE CLIENT TELL YOU WHAT PROBLEMS TO SOLVE

For a start, let's consider the basics: Who's doing most of the talking in this call? That's right. The salesperson. And he shouldn't be. The general rule of thumb in any sales call is what's called the 80/20 rule—you should be doing about 20 percent of the talking, and the client should be doing 80 percent. There's quite a bit of flexibility here, it's true, but if you find yourself dominating the conversation, you're doing something wrong.

The way out of this situation is pretty simple, and it's the most basic sales technique I've taught during the past 30 years: start asking questions.

In the beginning it almost doesn't matter what the questions are. Ask anything:

- Ask the client's relations with the rest of the industry.

- Query the client's business practices.

- Ask for a review of her inventory and how she determines what to keep in her warehouse.

These or a myriad of other questions will do the essential thing you want to do in an interview and what the salesperson in the scenario has singularly refused to do: get the client talking. Once you do that, the tone and dynamic of the conversation will shift. Rather than telling the client what to do about his business, you'll find that he's telling you what's wrong with it and asking for your help in fixing it.

That's the situation you want to be in.

The questions you ask should be open. In other words, they should require more than a yes or no answer. Your real object is to get the client to talk about the problems he sees in his business and how what you're selling can fix them.

A second problem with the sales call in the scenario is that the salesperson is dominating the discussion and clearly controlling the interview. You may say, "Well, what's wrong with that? After all, shouldn't the salesperson control the interview?"

Yes, but not in such an obvious way and not at the expense of the client. Control, after all, doesn't mean saying more words than the other person. It's not a contest. Control means determining the direction of the discussion and calling the turns in the conversation.

The third problem in the scenario is that the salesperson thinks he knows more about the client's problem than the client does. That's unlikely, since no one knows the inside of the client's business better than he does, but let's suppose for a moment that it's true. After all, salespeople are very intelligent, and I've never ceased to say that a salesperson should learn everything possible about the clients he's selling to.

But that doesn't mean you have to tell that to the client. No one, after all, likes a wiseass. And no one likes someone who barges in and starts telling people how to conduct their business. You wouldn't like it, would you?

All right then. Why do you think the client likes it?

Let's try it again.

Client: I don't know why we're talking this morning. There's no way you can possibly understand what we're going through.

Salesperson: I see. Why don't you tell me what you're going through, and then maybe we can figure out a way around it.

Client: Well, to start with, we're losing ground in the industry because everything's changing. We're providing the same kind of product we've always offered, but fewer people are buying it.

Salesperson: Why do you think that is?

Client: I don't know. That's what I want you to explain to me. What can we do to change that situation?

Salesperson: Well—

Client: So how are you going to help me?

Salesperson: I can show your employees how to deal with this kind of change. And once they can figure out what's really involved in the change, they can find a way to deal with it. And I'll help them through that process.

Client: I really don't know what you can do for me. The problem is with the entire industry, and you can't change that. Can't you find something that will improve my numbers right away?

Now the conversation at least has gotten off on the right foot. The salesperson is asking the right questions and is trying to figure out what's wrong. But there's still a problem here, and that's with the client.

FOCUS ON SPECIFIC SOLUTIONS

We've all had them: clients who don't really want the problem to be fixed. They're willing to tell you what's wrong, but they don't want a solution; instead, they want a sympathetic ear.

Anyone who sells services gets used to this kind of client, because they're particularly drawn to a salesperson who seems to deal in abstract narrative. They want a specific quick fix to the problem they're facing. In this case, the decline in revenue numbers has placed the executive who's the client in the sales call in a delicate position. He needs to convince his boss that he's got the situation under control while at the same time figuring out what the real problem is.

From the salesperson's point of view this can be extremely frustrating because it seems difficult to find anything to hold onto. The first thing to do is to explain to the client that change is the new normal for any business environment. This is a very difficult moment, because what any business craves, above all, is stability. No entrepreneur wants to hear you say, "So the first thing you're going to have to deal with is that everything's changing in your industry and it's transforming the way you do business." The client's natural reaction is going to be to duck and cover. She wants you to fix the problem she's got right now, not listen to a philosophical discourse on where the industry is going and why. But you can't get sucked into this. You have to focus on why the service you're providing is going to improve her life both in the immediate and long-term future. The best way to do this is to focus on specifics. Let's rerun the scenario as if you're selling the client legal services.

Client: What can you do for me? I don't need you to tell me what my problems are. I need you to show me how you'll approach my legal situation in a way that's going to make me feel secure that I can continue doing business.

Salesperson: I understand. But why don't you tell me what you think the challenges of your business are right now and why you'd need someone to help you with them?

Client: Well, the biggest issue is our liability guarantee. It seems as though in today's world we're being asked to guarantee that our widgets will have a shelf life of at least five years. But given the current state of the technology we've got in our plant, I'm not prepared to guarantee them for more than three years.

Salesperson: That's certainly a challenge. And I hope we can work together to find a solution. My firm has spent the past 10 years concentrating its efforts on business liability. We're very confident that once you understand the new legal guidelines around this issue we can find a way to make you feel more comfortable with it.

Client: Is that something you'd be willing to back up with specific terms in the contract?

Salesperson: Yes. Let's turn to our boilerplate here and look at Section III. . . .

Now we're getting there. We're no longer talking about all the things that can go wrong but about particular solutions to the client's problem. Here's where it counts to be specific. The more concrete and detailed you can be, the more able you are to overcome clients' particular questions and concerns. However, and this is an essential point, you shouldn't offer any firm guarantees or commitments until you've had a chance to check them with your front office. You don't want to be put in a position of agreeing to something that your company isn't willing to back up.

Here's also an instance in which selling a service differs from selling a product, while at the same time it's the same.

With a product, you can point to particular physical features that will do what the client wants. You can tell him very confidently that if he needs his widgets to fry eggs in 20 minutes or less, your widget has been tested to fry eggs in 15 minutes with a 95 percent success rate. That's the kind of detail a client loves to hear.

But how about with services? Here you need to stand on your record.

- How many clients have you serviced in the past?

- What was your success rate?

- By what percentage did you improve their business?

- What did this translate into in terms of dollars of top- and bottom-line revenue?

If you have these examples at your fingertips, you don't have to be caught up in the game of making commitments to the client that you may not be able to fulfill. You have to let him see that your history itself implies a particular level of success. Once you've gotten to that point, you can pull out the contract—as our imaginary salesperson has done in the preceding scenario—and start to go into the details of the deal. Those details will reinforce the implied promise and will keep the client looking forward to what you can do for him.

SELL ON THE
END RESULT

In a purely amateur spirit, I enjoy cooking. I'm a passionate dev-
otee of the various cooking channels to be found on cable television, and I'll spend hours watching chefs competing against one
another or standing behind a counter while an entranced studio
audience watches them chop, sauté, mince, and chiffonade. (I threw
in a couple of those terms just to prove to you that I know what
sauté and *chiffonade* mean. I'm not above boasting.)

I particularly enjoy baking and watching other people bake.
There's something magical to me about the fact that you can toss
eggs, butter, sugar, flour, and baking soda into a bowl, mix it, and
pour it into a greased pan. Then, after you put it into an oven (usually heated to 350 degrees), a chemical process transforms it. It
turns into something completely different.

It becomes cake.

Sometimes my cakes work, and sometimes they don't. I don't
claim to be Julia Child or Jacques Pépin (again, that's a little foodie
knowledge meant to impress you). But I understand that in baking, what counts is not necessarily what the batter looks like beforehand but what it looks like when it comes out of the oven. In
short, I cook for the result.

The same is true of selling. Like making a cake, it isn't always clean; sometimes it gets very messy, and the collective ingredients, before they go into the oven, may occasionally look unappetizing. But when a sale comes out of the oven, so to speak, it's done. And what counts is the result.

There are two interconnected points here, which are the subject of this chapter, "Sell on the End Result."

1. First, you sell on the result in the sense that the ultimate goal of your sale is to get a result: an inked contract. How you get there may not always be straightforward, and the path may get very confused and messy, but what really counts is getting to that end point.

2. The second point is that in your sales pitch, you must emphasize to the client that what counts *in your deal* is the result. Occasionally clients lose track of this and want to focus on the process itself. Your job is to get them back on track. They shouldn't be worried about what the cake looks like going into the oven; instead, they need to concentrate on what it's going to look like coming out.

Of course, I'm not naive about these matters, either as a salesperson or as a baker. Garbage in, garbage out, as the saying goes. If you don't do things right when you're preparing the batter, the cake will come out a disaster. But we can't get all hung up on appearances in the early stage of things. We've got to concentrate—and get the client to concentrate—on what we want to happen at the end of the process.

In selling services, this takes on particular importance because it's only at the end of the process, when the cake comes out of the oven, that the client will be able to understand fully what she's purchased from you. Services are judged entirely by their results;

after all, prior to that there's not much to look at. If, for instance, you're selling accounting services, your client may be momentarily impressed if your accountants show up every day, ready to go to work, and put in full eight-hour days. What's really going to wow her, though, is at the end of the fiscal year when she finds out that purchasing your service has saved her company $150,000. That's definitely a cake worth buying.

THE RECIPE FOR EFFECTIVE SALES CALLS

To get this result there are some specific things you can do:

1. **Start by selling the result.** No one wants to bake a cake until they know what it is they'll be eating at the end of the job. That's why cookbooks have all those glossy pictures of food, looking mouth-wateringly delicious, shot in soft focus, and usually presented against a background of luxurious dining. The authors are selling you the result—not what you'll see at the start of your efforts but what you'll be eating at the end. In the same way, when you're selling a service, start with what benefits it will bring to the client. After all, that's what the client is most interested in; that's why you're making a pitch in the first place.

2. **Outline a step-by-step process.** In order for the client to know what she's buying, you need to show exactly how the process will work. It's exactly like a recipe: Give her a series of steps, each one leading logically from the previous step and moving the process forward. You want to show her how you get from where she is now to the result you promised her at the beginning of the pitch.

3. **Make sure the elements all work together.** Imagine, if you will, baking a delicious apple tart. You've rolled out

the pastry dough, sliced the apples thin, and tossed them in sugar and cinnamon with a pinch of salt. You're getting ready to assemble them in the tart shell. And then, suddenly . . . layer the bottom of the shell with Boston baked beans.

Wha . . . ? No. No way. An alien element has been introduced. If you do that, the tart will be ruined.

In the same way, make sure that all the various parts of your presentation work together. Everything you talk to the client about should have a logical place in the framework of the sale. You can't afford for something to strike a false note.

4. **Include quality control.** Any good chef will tell you, you can't cook well unless you're willing to constantly taste. That's why, when you see professional chefs cooking up close, you'll constantly see them sticking spoons into sauces, checking the taste, then adding a dash of salt or pepper or perhaps a few quick squeezes of lemon juice. A chef who serves a dish to his customers that he's not quality checked throughout the cooking will find himself with an empty restaurant very swiftly.

In the same way, you as a salesperson must always be aware that your client will need constant monitoring. This is never truer than when you're selling services. As I've said, ultimately the client will judge you on the result. So you must be able to judge precisely how that result will come out. You must be absolutely confident that if you're selling a cleaning service to a large corporation, at the end of the month when you check in with the client, he won't tell you that there are dust bunnies the size of Cleveland behind the water cooler and the sinks in the bathroom haven't been scrubbed in two weeks.

You've got to show the client—and yourself—that there's a reliable and efficient system of quality control in place.

5. **Set final benchmarks.** The proof of the pudding, as some-
    one remarked long ago, is in the eating. Ultimately, your cli-
    ent is going to want a promise of specific results. Although, as
    I've indicated, you must be careful to clear contractual com-
    mitments with your home office, the contract for a service
    will set a series of conditions that you'll have to meet. You
    should take the initiative in setting these benchmarks and in
    making clear your commitment to meeting each of them.

TAKING THE COMPLETED CONTRACT OUT OF THE OVEN

There's something of the showman in me; I probably wouldn't be
in sales if that weren't true. So I confess to a good deal of pleasure
when, at a dinner party, I pull the finished product from the oven,
throw a sprinkling of icing sugar over the top, and take it to the
table to receive the plaudits of the guests. After all, there's nothing
as sweet as success.

In the same way, one of the triumphant moments of selling a
service is when, at the end of the contract, you can pull out the
results and trumpet them in front of your assembled audience. This
is an important moment because it's your proof to the clients that
they made the right decision in hiring you. The intangible object
you sold them has brought tangible benefits, ones that can now be
measured in dollars and cents.

It's also significant because it's the opportunity to resell the
service. After all, if it worked once, chances are it will continue
working. And the clients' confidence has been reinforced, in the
same way that my dinner guests know that the next time they
come back to chez Schiffman for a meal, they'll be treated to an
equally excellent dinner.

This is an essential point about service, and one any restaura-
teur will attest to: consistency is everything.

In a restaurant, if you serve a duck confit or a boeuf bourguignon to one set of customers, you must be sure that the next time you serve those dishes, customer number two will have exactly the same dining and taste experience as customer number one did. That's what keeps people coming back. No one wants to walk into a restaurant and not be sure, from night to night, whether she's going to get fine dining or the slops left out for the cat. In any establishment, consistency is the secret to success (always assuming, of course, that the restaurant is consistently good).

In the same way, if you've provided good service to a client for 12 months, you've got to be sure that you'll be able to provide the same sterling service for the next 12 months. That's the guarantee you make to everyone who comes to you: you will offer exactly the same quality service, no matter who the client.

Some companies fail precisely because they don't observe this rule. They're inconsistent in one of two ways, either of which is disastrous:

1. They offer varying levels of service, depending on the time of year, the resources available, or what they feel like on a Tuesday afternoon. The same level of attention to the needs of the client has to be provided every minute of every day. Otherwise, you'd better plan on finding some other way to make a living.

2. They offer varying levels of service depending on the perceived importance of the client. This is highly offensive as well as being generally bad business practice. The assumption of anyone selling a service must be that every client is equally important. That's one of the golden rules of service selling, and I urge you never to forget it.

In your final review for the year, when you go over with the client how things went, what was good, what could use improvement, and so on, it's important to quantify those benchmarks you set, to show the degree to which you met each one. Never try to blow smoke at the client and pretend you did something if you didn't. These meetings are brutally honest, and all falsity will be squeezed to the surface at the fiscal year's end.

If you're straightforward and focus on the end result, I guarantee your cakes will come out of the oven looking perfect every time.

CLIENT CHALLENGE: "I DON'T NEED THAT!"

Let's listen in on a portion of a sales call. Jennifer, the salesperson, is talking to Maxine, the buyer for a medium-size electronics firm with branches on the East Coast. This is Jennifer's first pitch to Maxine.

Jennifer: What I think is interesting about our product offering this season is that we have adopted a policy of guaranteeing service representatives make on-site visits in the event of problems within 18 hours to select cities during periods of heavy traffic, such as from November through the end of December. The normal cost of those service calls is discounted.

Maxine: That is an impressive benefit. How much is the discount?

Jennifer: It depends on the city and the volume of product, but it can be as much as 60 percent.

Maxine: Which cities exactly are involved in this program?

Jennifer: Well, the program is focused right now on cities nearest us. So the main cities involved are Chicago, Cleveland, St. Louis, Cincinnati, Detroit, Toledo, and Indianapolis. We plan to expand outward somewhat over the next year or so.

Maxine: What would the discount be on cities on the East Coast?

Jennifer: We haven't extended the program to them, since the cost of service calls to those areas doesn't make it possible for us to discount them to any great extent.

Maxine: I see. But my outlets are mostly in the Boston–New York corridor, so it doesn't sound as if I'd benefit much from this.

Jennifer: Well, but you have plans to expand further, don't you?

Maxine: Possibly at some point in the future, but—

Jennifer: See, that's really the point at which the program would have a significant impact on your P&L. You'd be looking at some serious discounts.

Maxine: Yes, but we're not—

Jennifer: I mean, you guys really have to think about the future and about the best way to build in expansion possibilities for your business.

Maxine: I don't think you understand. What I'm concerned about is the situation we have right now, not in the future.

Jennifer: Well, it just seems to me that this is a pretty narrow-minded way to think of your business. What I can offer—

Maxine: Listen to me very carefully, Jennifer. I don't need what you're trying to sell me. And I don't like your attitude. This meeting is over.

That was a disaster, wasn't it? It's a shame, too, because the idea of a shipping discount during holidays is a very attractive one, and it's one that would probably have a huge impact on the ability of a salesperson to close deals—but only if (and here's the important part!) *it actually benefits the client.*

This is where everything starts to go wrong for Jennifer. She's so enamored of what her company is offering that she's not thinking about Maxine's situation as a company located on the East Coast. When Maxine calls this rather obvious situation to her attention, rather than step back and focus on what she can offer that Maxine wants, Jennifer does the worst possible thing: She doubles down on her original offer.

REALIZE THE CLIENT KNOWS HER BUSINESS BEST

This is an error I've seen salespeople make time and time again, and it seems worse, for some reason, when they're selling a service rather than a physical product. The client tells them, often in so many words, that she doesn't need what they're selling, and they don't believe her.

Now this is tricky, because there are often times when a client doesn't realize that the service you're offering could benefit her. She determines, possibly on the basis of inadequate information, that she doesn't need it. With some finesse, you can still close the deal. You do this not by arguing with her outright, but by offering her further information that will convince her of the value of what you're selling.

Jennifer, in the scenario, doesn't do that. Instead, she takes the worst possible tactic and starts to argue with the client. Going down this road creates a number of problems:

- It implies that you, the salesperson, think you know the client's business and industry better than she knows it (this may be true, but no one likes being told that outright).

- It sets up a negative dynamic between the two of you, one in which you're pushing the client to do something she doesn't want to do, rather than leading her gently in the direction of something that she does want to do.

- It cuts off any flow of information from the client, since she assumes that you'll use anything she says against her in an effort to reinforce your position.

Jennifer compounds the problem by her use of aggressive terms such as *narrow-minded*. Again, I stress that this kind of thing has nothing to do with the objective reality of Maxine's business. Jennifer may very well be right: Maxine's future expansion will quite possibly be toward the Midwest, in which case discounted service to those areas will be a powerful benefit. But any sort of emotionally charged language is going to do exactly what it did in this case: cut off the sales call. Jennifer is out the door before she quite knows what's happened to her, and, in all likelihood, Maxine's next phone call is going to be to Jennifer's boss, telling him never to send Jennifer to meet with her again.

ADAPT TO MEET THE CLIENT'S NEEDS

Let's think about how this discussion could have gone. Let's imagine that Jennifer is a graduate of the Schiffman School of Sales Theory and knows that in any circumstance where you run into client resistance you should do the following things:

- Start asking questions.

- Encourage the client to explain her or his resistance.

- With the aid of these two techniques, identify the problem or problems causing the resistance.

- Determine a possible solution to the problem that you and your company can offer.

- Present the solution to the client.

Assuming that she's thoroughly absorbed these lessons, here's how Jennifer might have handled Maxine's comments.

Jennifer: What I think is interesting about our product offering this season is that we have adopted a policy of guaranteeing service representatives make on-site visits in the event of problems within 18 hours to select cities during periods of heavy traffic, such as from November through the end of December. The normal cost of those service calls is discounted.

Maxine: Which cities are involved?

Jennifer: Well, the program is focused right now on cities nearest us. So the main cities involved are Chicago, Cleveland, St. Louis, Cincinnati, Detroit, Toledo, and Indianapolis. We plan to expand outward somewhat over the next year or so.

Maxine: So you're only discounting cities in the Midwest? Sorry, I don't need that.

Jennifer: I see. Could you tell me why this wouldn't benefit you?

Maxine: Well, we're exclusively located in the New York–Boston area, so that sort of thing wouldn't help me at all.

Jennifer: Does the company have plans to expand in the near future?

Maxine: We're planning to expand in the next year, but we haven't decided the form that expansion will take.

Jennifer: I see. Am I correct in thinking that service costs are a significant element for you in deciding on a vendor?

Maxine: Yes, very much so.

Jennifer: So what would help make a difference to you in terms of those kinds of costs?

Maxine: Well, I suppose what I'd really like would be a discount along the lines of what you're offering, but for coastal cities.

Jennifer: Interesting. If we were able to do those kinds of discounts—and with our present program, these can add up to almost 60 percent—would you be willing to look at substantially larger orders?

Maxine: Maybe. It would depend on the amount of the discount.

Jennifer: One thing that would be a big help to me is if you could indicate to me how long a service rep normally takes to come to one of your facilities.

Maxine: Our current vendor guarantees 18 hours.

Jennifer: Is that with no discount?

Maxine: Right.

Jennifer: Well, I'll have to talk this over with my boss. But I think we might be able to help you. If you could guarantee an increased volume of orders and a grace period of 24 hours for the service rep to make the call, I think we could offer a similar discount to the one we're offering for cities in the Midwest.

Maxine: I'll have to think about that. It's an interesting proposal.

Jennifer: Sure, I understand. And, as I say, I've got to talk this over with my boss. Why don't I call you next Tuesday morning, and we can discuss it some more and hopefully work out a solution that benefits both of us? Is 10 a.m. okay for a phone call?

Now we're getting somewhere. Jennifer has focused the conversation on how to benefit Maxine. She's not just pushing her discount program—instead, she's adapting it to fit the client's needs. A couple of additional things to note:

1. Jennifer tries to get as much information as possible from Maxine before offering a solution. This example is pretty compressed, given the space considerations of this book; in real life the conversation would probably have gone on quite a bit longer, with Jennifer working to extract specific facts and figures from Maxine about the kind of service she's receiving from her current vendor and the kinds of discounts that would help change her mind. But the absolutely essential thing is to keep the client talking.

2. Jennifer does not make an up-front guarantee; rather, she proposes a possible solution but makes it contingent on discussions with her boss. I've said the same thing elsewhere: don't make commitments you may not be able to keep. It's much better to take the time to confirm that your company can make this deal.

3. Jennifer ends the discussion by setting up a specific time and place to continue things. In circumstances like this, it's essential to keep the dialogue going, and Jennifer's suggestion of a 10 a.m. Tuesday phone call does precisely that.

Even with these considerations in mind, sometimes when clients say no to a service, they mean no. The best thing you can do under those circumstances is accept it and move on. With luck you've got some other things to sell them. But if you follow Jennifer's sales technique in the second example, you'll succeed in turning around some situations in which your client's initial reaction is, "I don't need that."

THE BENEFITS OF INTANGIBLES

5

S ome things just can't be seen. They can't be touched. They can't be tasted, felt, or heard. Nonetheless, we couldn't do without them. Let me give you an example.

A while back, I was preparing a presentation for an important conference. I'd been invited to give a keynote, and I was as nervous as a schoolgirl before her first prom. The conference was 10 days away, and I found that I couldn't sleep. I couldn't eat. I was having regular nightmares, during which I'd toss off the blankets and kick down the sheets.

My wife, not unreasonably, brought this to my attention. "Look," she said, "you're obviously bothered by something. And it's keeping both of us up at night. Get help for whatever's plaguing you, or you and I are going to start sleeping in different parts of the house." There was nothing threatening about this; it was just a simple statement of fact.

I considered what she'd said and then went to consult a friend. We met over drinks in a bar in midtown Manhattan.

I explained to him that for some reason I'd had insomnia. I suspected that it had to do with the presentation I was scheduled to give, but I couldn't go beyond that. After all, it wasn't as if I'd never talked before a group of people before. I was quite used to it, in fact. So I didn't see why that should bother me to any degree. However, for whatever reason, I was tossing and turning during the night. What was the problem?

My friend, with the benefit of an outside opinion, considered matters for a while in silence. Then he asked, "What are you afraid of?"

I replied, confidently, "Nothing."

"Really?"

"No, really. Nothing."

There was an uncomfortable silence. Then I dug a bit deeper and admitted, "All right, there's something."

"What?"

The bar around us was noisy, so I leaned up to his ear and said, "I'm afraid of failing."

In that moment of saying those four simple words, I found an immense sense of relief. I realized later that this was the problem that had been plaguing me for three solid weeks, during which I'd disrupted my own life as well as my wife's. Fear of failure had been a crushing, all-consuming concern, and it wasn't until I admitted it to someone else that I was able to confront it and come to grips with it.

It also occurred to me, when I thought about the situation with the benefit of several months' hindsight, that my fear had been a chimera. There wasn't anything specific for me to be afraid of. After all, I'd dealt with the specifics of business decisions before. I'd talked to numerous people, who'd given me just about every conceivable reaction I could expect. So what, really, was I afraid of?

I was terrified of something that was abstract, something that I'd never stood up to before. In short, I was afraid of an intangible.

Oddly enough, this experience pushed me to confront the problem of intangibles in selling. It's one that I'd encountered before but had never really met and resolved. But I realized that one of the features of selling a service is that you're selling something that is an unknown. It's a bit scary—like my fear of failure. And therefore, we have to meet it head on and figure it out. Otherwise it defeats us.

DEFINING INTANGIBLES

When you sell a service, you're selling a promise. That's key to making the sale. You're not selling a particular object; instead, you're selling a future commitment, an agreement to do something with a future benefit. For instance, when you sell accounting services, what you're really selling is the promise that at some point in the future these services will save your client money. You are saying, in effect, "You may not realize any specific benefit right now, your inventory may not increase in asset value at the moment we make this sale, but you'll realize its benefits later."

To conclude this sale, the first thing you've got to do is put a monetary value on what you're selling. You've got to value what you sell. In the preceding example, you've got to illustrate specifically how much money your client will save by going with your accounting scheme. No abstractions will do here. It must be framed in terms of dollars and cents. If you're thinking about offering a cleaning service, your offer must be in terms of how much money it can save your client every week. How much will it cost for you to clean his office, as opposed to having his disgruntled staff do it every Saturday morning? Once you can put a dollar-per-hour figure on it, you're much closer to closing the negotiation.

I think—after long, careful consideration—that this is one of the big problems salespeople have with selling services. Somehow, what they're selling doesn't seem real. And the solution, as I constantly tell them, is to make it real. Make it specific, make it concrete, make it cost dollars and cents.

I've said before that when you sell, you're addressing someone who has a problem. Every client has some problem he or she is trying to solve. Otherwise, clients wouldn't be listening to you.

They believe that what you're selling will help them overcome that problem.

When you sell a tangible object, you can calculate exactly how it will help them. For instance, if I sell a thousand widgets to Joe at Big Box Company, I know he needs the widgets (otherwise, of course, why would we even be having this conversation?). I can measure how much he needs it in terms of the profit margin he'll be making per widget. It becomes very easy to quantify the problem and the solution.

DEMONSTRATING SPECIFIC BENEFITS

But how do you quantify something like a cleaning service? If I'm selling my company's ability to go in once every two days and clean my client's offices from top to bottom, what's the best way to demonstrate that this service represents a matter of dollars to him? What, really, does it cost a client not to have a clean office?

This is the fundamental fear that most salespeople who specialize in selling services confront: that they won't be able to demonstrate a specific benefit. I have the following points of advice:

1. **Set a scenario in which your company *doesn't* provide the service you're selling.** For instance, if you're selling cleaning services, describe what will happen to the client's office if it's not cleaned. Be sure to stress the way in which that will affect all aspects of his business, including his client relationships, his ability to attract new clients, the threat of disease or accidents caused by filthy working conditions, and so on. The more graphic this is, the more the client is likely to understand the consequences.

2. **Refer to the benefits you've provided other clients.** We all like to see ourselves in other people's situations, and

if you can find someone from your client list—you don't, naturally, need to mention any names—who is in the situation of your potential client, you can show how you helped turn his or her business around.

3. **Focus on a specific set of measurable benchmarks.** One of the great challenges facing those who sell services is finding ways to measure what they provide. But you should come into any sales call with a very clear set of goals you'll be able to reach and a timetable by which you'll be able to meet them. Otherwise the client will rapidly be convinced you're just trying to blow smoke in his face, and you'll get nowhere fast.

4. **Present your client with statistics, based on past performance, of what your services have meant in terms of revenue and profitability gains for your clients.** This is by far the hardest thing you'll have to come up with, because those numbers have to be convincing; you can't pull them out of thin air. Nonetheless, you should be able to quantify what your service means to the client.

The disadvantage of selling something that's intangible is that it's, well, intangible. The client won't know about its benefits until some point in the future, and those advantages often seem abstract. However, you should keep in mind that the advantage of selling intangibles is that they're . . . intangible. This situation allows you to stress the extent to which this service has benefited other clients and to offer various scenarios about how it can benefit the client. And, best of all, those scenarios haven't happened yet. They're in the future, and the client can imagine how they'll play out. All in all, that's not a bad situation to be in.

The thing that I want you to come away with from this chapter is this: An intangible is a possibility. It's a benefit that hasn't yet happened. As such, you can let the client's imagination work on what it will do for his or her business, supported on a scaffolding of statistics and numbers. It's possible, naturally, that the client's imagination will veer off into some nightmare scenario in which everything goes wrong. But your job as a salesperson is to head that sort of thing off at the pass and instead patiently guide him into a happy meadow in which all is sweetness and light. Don't be dishonest; never be dishonest with a client. But focus on the positive and let him realize the benefits.

"BUT CAN'T I DO THAT MYSELF?"

6

There's a story—it might be apocryphal, I don't know—about a tech support guy who was sitting at work one day when the phone rang.

"Hello, this is Mike in tech support. How can I help you?"

"Uh, hi. I've got a problem with my computer. Can you tell me what to do?"

"Sure. What seems to be the problem?"

"Well, the coffee cup holder on my machine doesn't seem to be working."

The tech shook his head to clear his ears. He removed his headset and blew into the earpiece.

"I'm sorry," he said. "Did you say your . . . uh . . ."

"Yeah, my coffee cup holder on the side of my computer. It doesn't seem to be working anymore."

The tech felt a faint throbbing start around his temples. Keeping his voice very calm, he said, "I'm sorry, sir, but I don't know of any computers that come equipped with coffee cup holders."

"Sure you do," the voice on the other end said cheerily. "It just pops right out of the side of the machine."

The throbbing was getting worse. The tech took a deep breath.

"This coffee cup holder," he asked, "is it flat, with a hole in the middle?"

"Yeah, that's right."

"That's your CD-ROM drive, sir. You don't use it for coffee cups."

Every person who works in customer service has stories to repeat about goofy questions or requests. I suspect, though I've never worked in customer service, that they sit around after work, with their feet up on their desks, trading stories about who had the stupidest or weirdest question during the day. I have a lot of sympathy for these people, because in the face of what sometimes seems to be a toxic cloud of confusion and hostility from their clients, they have to remain calm and professional and find a solution. In fact, there's a valuable lesson for salespeople in their work, because any customer service person worth his salt will tell you that when a client calls, the first thing you should do is to start asking questions.

THOU SHALT ASK QUESTIONS

This is Schiffman's first commandment: Thou shalt ask questions.

The second commandment (actually, I don't have these things in a particular order—they're just jotted down on bits of paper and in miscellaneous folders on my computer desktop as they've occurred to me over the years) is this: Thou shalt not, under any circumstances, be condescending or rude to the client.

Let's look at what happens when you don't ask questions and instead make assumptions, and, further, when you demean the client. Robert is a salesperson, selling computer tech services to Mark, an entrepreneur who's been selling equipment to fly fishermen and is planning to launch a website to expand his business online.

Robert: The most important thing for you is to establish yourself with a clear, strong online presence. That's where we can help you.

Mark: Right. I was thinking that I'd like to be able to reach people who like to fish when they're first looking to replenish their equipment in early spring.

Robert: No, that's too limited an approach. You've got to maintain a strong online presence all the time. Things are different now than when you probably started off in this business. You were selling out of a bricks-and-mortar operation, but now it's all about click-throughs. You can't just think seasonally anymore.

Mark: Well, could you give me some direction on how you think the website should look?

Robert: No problem. We can create a website for you that will allow you to constantly update content and penetrate the hobby fishing community.

Mark: So you'll create the site for me?

Robert: Yes, and we'll maintain it as well.

Mark: But couldn't I do that myself?

Robert: No, I don't think that would be a good idea. With something of this complexity—you'll see what I mean when I show you some of the sites we've set up for other businesses—it really takes a trained professional and not an amateur. There are a lot of ways to really screw up a site like this unless you really know what you're doing. Now why don't I just set up—

Mark: Excuse me, but I don't want to waste any more of your time. I don't think you're a good fit for our business. I appreciate your information, but we're all done.

Instead of Robert successfully reeling in the sale, Mark tossed him back without a second look. Why?

I can sum up Robert's mistakes in a single word: arrogance.

It's a sin that too many salespeople possess, and it's never forgiven. It's particularly germane to our discussion of selling services because it crops up there a lot. It's especially problematic in the computer industry, but I've seen it come up in other places as well.

Why is that? Well, think about it: When you sell a service, you're selling an ability that you and your company possess to do something that nobody else (except your competitors) can do well or wants to do at all. Your success depends to a great extent on your ability to perform this service better than anyone else. From that point, it's all too easy to think that you're such an expert and so good at doing this that everyone else is a bunch of yahoos who don't know their elbows from their assets. Tech people are particularly prone to this thinking, at least partly because of the speed with which the information revolution has developed. But they're not the only ones. In my time, I've known arrogant plumbers, accountants, carpenters, and television repair people. And don't even get me started on the arrogance that's often found in the medical and legal professions.

Robert is convinced that Mark knows nothing about computers or websites. That may be true. Mark himself may be quite willing to admit the limitations of his knowledge. But he doesn't like to be told it—by you or anyone else.

Moreover, Robert makes it very clear in this conversation that he wants the relationship between him and Mark to be a dependent one. Mark will be completely reliant upon Robert and his expertise not only in setting up the website but in maintaining and running it. In other words, Mark will have to turn over a significant aspect of his business to someone else, someone he doesn't yet know and has no reason to trust. That's not going to be something any self-respecting entrepreneur will do.

Finally, Robert isn't willing to recognize or admit the limitations of his own knowledge. He may know all about computers, websites, click-through rates, and so on, but Mark's the expert on the fishing community. Robert needs to start his sales pitch from that point—Mark knows what the fishing community wants. His problem is how to effectively reach them. That's the problem he and Robert must solve together.

RESPECT THE CLIENT'S EXPERTISE AND SOLVE PROBLEMS TOGETHER

With that in mind, let's see how the sales call could develop if Robert remembers to ask questions and to respect Mark's expertise and viewpoint.

Robert: From what you've been telling me, the most important goal you have right now is to establish yourself and your company in the fishing community with a clear, strong online presence. Is that right?

Mark: Yes, absolutely. We're starting to build a good local buzz in the community as a company that's got a lot of expertise about sport fishing, but we want to expand our reach.

Robert: Could you tell me something more about the community and what they expect from a website?

Mark: They're very committed. A sports fisherman will spend upwards of $5,000 to $10,000 on equipment. And they feel a strong interest in maintaining the environment, since it's good for the spawning of fish and the continuation of our sport. The average sport fisherman is male, about 35, and has a median income of around $65,000.

Robert: I see. What about your competition? Are there other sport fishing websites up there?

Mark: Yes, but I think we can successfully compete with them. One thing I'd like to see is for us to have a place where

SECRETS OF SELLING SERVICES

people can post comments and get into discussions about their experiences.

Robert: Sure. You mean forums?

Mark: Yeah, if that's what they're called. I'd also like a way for people to be able to rate particular pieces of equipment.

Robert: Absolutely. We can build that into the site without a problem. Coming back to the forums for a minute, do you want the discussion on them to be moderated?

Mark: What do you mean?

Robert: Well, a lot of forums have a moderator who makes sure that nothing inappropriate is posted, that posters don't get into arguments that get out of hand, and so on.

Mark: Could I do that myself?

Robert: Sure. But keep in mind that it can be a time sink. Especially if you build up a large, energetic community, you could have a lot of posts to go through.

Mark: What's your recommended solution?

Robert: I'd recommend approaching someone who's respected in the sport fishing community to moderate the board on a volunteer basis. Perhaps you could reward him with either some free equipment or a discount on equipment. That could help build the website's legitimacy in the sport community too.

Mark: That seems like a good solution.

What a difference! It's like night and day from the first discussion. Now, instead of trying to impress Mark with his knowledge and expertise in building and maintaining websites, Robert has done what any good salesperson should do. He's focused on helping the client with his problem.

Notice that when Mark suggests that he can do some element of tech service (in this case, moderating discussion forums) himself, Robert doesn't automatically dismiss this. Instead, he tells Mark that while it's possible, it will come with a cost—in this case, time. Then he suggests a reasonable solution, one that also speaks directly to Mark's need to build a good online reputation in the sport fishing community. It seems clear that at the end of this discussion Robert and Mark are going to be able to form a productive partnership.

Not every discussion goes so well. There are times when you'll have to tell a client that no, he really can't do it himself. But when a client brings up this argument, my recommendation is that you give a three-part answer. First, confirm that, yes, the client can do it himself. Second, point out the specific costs involved in this. Third, propose a solution in which even if he can't do it himself, he'll still be happy with what you propose.

SERVICES IN THE AGE OF THE INTERNET

7

I can well remember the day I discovered the Internet.

I had heard for some time about this mysterious entity called the World Wide Web, a network of connected computers that could apparently find anything and anyone. I was skeptical at first, like most people my age, but gradually, through ceaseless siege by younger colleagues, I decided to give it a whirl. I plugged my computer into my phone (we pretty much all had dial-up connections in those days), tapped away diligently, following the menu commands as well as the instructions of my younger nephew who was standing at my shoulder. Finally, a screen came up and, with what would today be regarded as painful slowness, a page loaded.

It was a revelation.

I don't know what I'd been expecting. What I'd definitely not been anticipating was the sheer scope of the thing. It seemed, to my entranced eyes, as if the whole world was on the web. (I know, I know. World Wide Web. I get it now.) There were hundreds of thousands of web addresses, and I wondered if someone was going to make a directory of them. (Today, of course, the number of URLs is in the hundreds of millions, and the idea of there being a single directory of them in the age of Google would strike any of my friends as hilarious.)

As I became more accustomed to using the Internet, and as it got progressively faster, I tried to grapple with what this meant for sales. The initial thoughts I had weren't very good. After all, I reasoned, if people could just go online and look up goods, why would they even need salespeople? Wouldn't they decide to cut out the middlemen entirely and move to a system of direct selling? Wouldn't that benefit both sellers and consumers?

THE AGE OF DIRECT SALES

There are still times when these questions pound at me with disturbing frequency. For instance, in 2011 the venerable bookstore chain Borders went belly-up. Years of mismanagement, contraction of the economy, and increasing competition from Barnes & Noble and especially the Internet giant Amazon.com destroyed the chain that had begun as a single bookstore in Ann Arbor, Michigan.

The conclusion arrived at by many of my friends in publishing was that Internet sales had destroyed brick-and-mortar stores. They pointed to Amazon as the future of book sales. They referred to the fact that with e-readers, one click of a button will get you a copy of a *New York Times* bestseller, within seconds and without having to leave the comfort of your armchair. Surely, they said, this is the wave of the future.

It may be that they're right. I don't know. As an old-fashioned sort of guy, I confess I still like the smell of a newly opened book, the scent of ink on fresh paper, and the feel of the pages as they turn beneath my hands. But maybe I'm behind the times.

One thing I've had to deal with, though, in my business, is the growth of online sales. Many have argued that my job as a trainer of salespeople is in danger of being overcome by the prevalence of online sales. Selling, in this viewpoint, is something that's practically obsolete. Offer a product to consumers, and they'll buy it, communicating its virtues to one another on message boards. In the words of that great (if somewhat weird) movie *Field of Dreams,* "Build it and they will come."

THE BASICS HAVEN'T CHANGED

To all this, I say, "Poppycock." There's still a need for salespeople, and there's still a need for the kind of sales training I and others provide. The reason is very simple: The basics of sales haven't changed. Only the format has.

But isn't the format so different that it's completely altered the game? This is a question I hear from a lot of young salespeople. Well, yes and no. It's true that we've got to get used to being closer to our customers, and we've got to deal with the fact that they communicate with the end consumer and with each other on an almost instantaneous basis. That can magnify the effects of any mistakes we make, which is pretty intimidating. But everything I've been preaching for the past 35 years still holds true:

- Ask questions to find out what the customer thinks he wants.

- Be positive and focus on the upside.

- Quantify the benefits of what you're selling.

- An objection is just an unrecognized opportunity.

All these principles continue to be valid, whether you're selling to a store, a company, an end consumer, or the buyer for a department-store chain—or over an Internet site.

If you are selling services, the Internet represents both a challenge and a chance. On the one hand, you have the opportunity to create a very impressive picture of what your services can do. I've seen websites on which the company selling services demonstrated with graphs, charts, and cartoon characters exactly what their people would do for a client and how it would increase the client's top and bottom lines. No question, the Internet can be a huge help when you're selling something abstract.

On the other hand, the Internet puts you one further step removed from your customers, whether they're the buyer for a store or the end consumer. You've interposed a computer screen between the two of you, and you won't be able to take it away. This can make an abstract process seem even further removed from reality.

THE VALUE OF ADDED VALUE

To overcome this challenge, there's one absolutely key ingredient: your Internet-based business must offer some benefit not available to brick-and-mortar stores. Amazon is really good at this. To their end consumers, they offer discounts on unit price as well as discounts on shipping. They also have a generally reliable customer relations policy that is focused on giving consumers what they want when they want it. For other businesses (for instance, publishers), they offer an extremely refined selling system in which each customer's Amazon page is attuned to what the customer wants (based on algorithms that calculate customer tastes from their previous purchases).

When it comes to selling services on the Internet, this approach offers huge advantages. Internet sales of services don't just have to mean sticking up a random web page listing what you do ("Snow removal! Guaranteed! Lowest prices anywhere!"). It offers you, instead, a chance to reach out to consumers and to draw on their feedback to improve your service.

THE IMPORTANCE OF CROWDSOURCING

Several years ago I became increasingly aware of a phenomenon called crowdsourcing. It was initially applied to computer programs such as Linux. Then other companies began to get in on the act, and before we knew where we were, crowdsourcing had become a standard feature of many companies' business strategies.

Essentially, crowdsourcing means that a company turns over some part of its R&D and marketing functions to its customers. It lets the customers help design the products they're going to buy. The advantages of this, if it's done right, are tremendous. After all, the customers are the end users of the product, so they have at least some idea of what they're looking for.

The idea can be taken too far, and has been on some occasions. But I think the concept is a sound one. And it's deeply connected to the Internet because the Internet is what allows customers to almost instantly communicate their opinions.

To take a small example, Amazon, from an early point in its existence, allowed customers to post reviews of the books it sells on its website. Not all of these reviews are good; in fact, a pretty high proportion of them can be bad, sometimes. But Amazon has decided that the issues with bad customer reviews are outweighed by the benefits of obtaining good ones. I find myself influenced by these reviews on occasion. If I'm mulling whether to buy a book or not, I'll probably look at the reviews and read a couple of them—usually a few of the five-star reviews, and several of the one-star reviews to get a range. Then, based partly on those reviews, I'll make a decision about whether to buy the book.

The concept here is remarkable. In effect, Amazon is permitting its customers to market its products.

This idea is even more important when it comes to services. When a physical product such as a book, a lawnmower, or a piece of machinery is involved, I can evaluate it myself based on its characteristics and how well they solve my problem. (I have a problem, or I wouldn't be buying the product.) But a service, because of its abstract nature, is harder to evaluate. So what better way to sell my service than to let my customers whom I've served speak up in favor of my service? Of course, not all the reviews are going to be glowing ones, but in general the good will outweigh the bad. They'd better, or I'm doing something seriously wrong and need to reevaluate my standards.

This leads me to a final point. One of the effects of the Internet has been to accelerate the building of communities. There's nothing new, naturally, in the concept of communities. People divide naturally into groups based on their interests and activities. But the Internet has made it a lot easier for such people to communicate with one another and to interact with each other.

From your point of view as a salesperson, the formation of these communities has both advantages and disadvantages.

The chief advantage is that it makes it far easier to spread the word about the service you're selling. If you create something that solves a significant problem for someone in your industry, chances are that in a very short time everyone else in the industry is going to hear about it.

There are, however, two important disadvantages that spring from this.

First, if you do something wrong, everyone's going to hear about it right away. Something well done will create ripples in the pond of human communication; a mistake can set off a tidal wave. So if there are defects in the service you're selling, don't think for a minute that you can keep them to yourself. Everyone's going to know about them, and a lot faster than you think.

Second, if your service is innovative and effective, your competition will hear about it almost instantaneously. The age of the Internet has upped the ante for competition among businesses, and as a salesperson on the front lines, you have to be prepared to sell rapidly developing services. According to Moore's Law, the number of transistors that can be placed on an integrated circuit doubles every two years. That means technology is increasing at an almost incredible pace, and you're going to have to keep up with it.

So welcome to the Internet Age. Not for the faint of heart, but one from which you can reap unimaginable rewards.

"HOW DO YOU KNOW WHAT I WANT?"

8

True story. Really.

Several holiday seasons ago I was stuck with the age-old question husbands have been asking for about 2,000 years: What do I get my wife for Christmas?

We've been married for a lot of years, and you'd think that this sort of thing would get easier. After all, as time goes by spouses know one another better, and it would seem self-evident that you'd understand more about one another's tastes. You'd have a better idea of what your spouse really wants to find under the Christmas tree on December 25, and you could just go out to the store (or, these days, sit down at the computer) and get it.

That's what you'd think.

In point of fact, I find the problem more complicated. After all, as a result of years of gift giving my wife has practically everything she wants or needs. Not being a woman given to extravagance, she doesn't constantly dream up strange wants or needs, and so the biggest issue for me every year is, what do I give a woman who apparently has everything?

Some Christmases ago, I hit on what I thought was the perfect gift. I'm not going to tell you what it was except that it was expensive, exclusive, and I had to order it in August to be sure it would be ready for delivery by the holiday season. I was very proud of myself and took the liberty of self-congratulations leading up to Christmas. Round about Thanksgiving, I started hinting delicately that she should expect something pretty special under the tree this year.

My wife, who has a much better idea of my gift-buying capacities than I do, sensibly said nothing and waited. I increased the hints, but she wouldn't take the bait.

Finally, the day arrived. We sat around in our pajamas on Christmas morning, opening gifts while the coffeepot perked contentedly in the background. At the right moment, I laid my present on her lap.

She pried open the wrapping paper (my wife is one of those compulsive people who saves wrapping paper from year to year) and gazed at the contents. She said nothing.

Finally, I said, "Hope you like it, honey."

She smiled, carefully and slowly, and said, "Of course, dear. It's just what I wanted."

From her look and tone, I realized that the big buildup had, in fact, ended in disappointment. I felt as if I wanted to sink through the floor.

Later, when our emotions had cooled a bit and we'd gotten past the strain of the holidays, I sought guidance from her. How had I laid such an egg? She smiled, patted me on my bald spot, and said, "How do you know what I want?"

There's a profound sales lesson here—one that I've been trying to pound into salespeople for the past three and a half decades. Let's see how this unfolds in a sales call.

Roger, a confident and energetic salesperson, is trying to sell a line of software products to C.J., a vice president of an up-and-coming small publishing company.

Roger: I think the main thing to recommend our software is its versatility. For example—and I've got some recommendations on this I'd like to show you later—it can provide you with a significant access to point-of-sale data as well as the ability to analyze your return rates on product.

C.J.: That's great, but what we really need in our business right now is something that can do inventory tracking.

Roger: I don't think that's really essential for you at this stage of your business. I have a lot of clients in publishing; you can see that from our client list on our website, and I also have a lot of contacts in the publishing industry. I've investigated your existing inventory software, and what I'm being told is that it's pretty much what you need to do the job. Anyway, we don't really make that kind of product.

C.J.: But—

Roger: Wouldn't it be worthwhile for you to have a system in place that could tell you the levels of your profitability on individual titles, particularly on a week-to-week basis?

C.J.: Sure, but—

Roger: And I think you'll find that our service package beats what you've got in place by quite a substantial margin as well. For example, we can guarantee that a service rep will respond to any issues or problems with the software within a 5-hour margin. Your current vendor offers service within 24 hours.

C.J.: We're actually pretty happy with them. In fact, we've been working with them for—

Roger: It's not really a question of having a long relationship. What you need to ask yourself is, what are you getting out of that relationship? And I'm happy to show you some figures, which I have right here, that will indicate that your current vendor is costing you up to $25,000 a year in additional costs, costs that you'd save if you go with the package I'm recommending.

C.J.: Well, I don't know. I'll take it up with the board . . .

Now, you may think that Roger has the better of this exchange. After all, seemingly at the end C.J. pretty much seems to be saying she'll recommend a sale to the board. But, in fact, leaving aside for a minute whether C.J. is actually likely to make such a recommendation in light of the conversation, what's the real problem here?

The answer is that Roger, throughout this discussion, hasn't actually learned anything about C.J.'s business. He's based his whole pitch on a series of assumptions that may or may not be true. And one fully expects C.J. to say to him, at some point, "How do you know what I want?"

The answer, sadly, is that Roger doesn't. He think he does, but he's forgotten one of the basic rules of sales technique: you don't know what your client wants until she tells you. The pity of it is that Roger is doing so many things right in this pitch. He's got a lot of the facts and figures about C.J.'s company down pat, and he clearly knows the industry and a lot about the company and the competition. But these things alone aren't going to save this sales call if Roger won't ask questions.

There's also the fact of Roger's hectoring, bullying style. I'm all for strong, positive selling—in fact, I've written an entire book on the subject: *The Power of Positive Selling*. But positive selling doesn't mean riding roughshod over the client. What Roger displays in his approach is a lack of respect for C.J. and a lack of interest in her opinions and insights. That might get you somewhere in the short run; in the long run, it's deadly.

LEARN WHAT THE CLIENT WANTS BY ASKING AND LISTENING

Now, let's imagine how things might have turned out if Roger had thought to ask questions instead of spouting facts and figures.

Roger: While I think that one of the great things about our software is its versatility, I'd really like to find out some more about exactly what it is you need from a software program for your business.

C.J.: Well, we need an inventory tracking system. We don't really have anything right now that meets our needs. And we're interested in being able to analyze POS data.

Roger: I think I could help with that. Tell me about your customer base.

C.J.: We cater to a younger, hipper readership. A lot of our authors are bloggers who build up a substantial audience before we publish their books. And we're trying to get into e-books more, trying to stay on the crest of the wave.

Roger: That's great. I think we can help you there. What inventory tracking system do you currently have in place?

C.J.: We're using Excel spreadsheets that have to be manually updated, so we tend to fall behind. Also they're subject to a lot of data entry errors. What I'd like is something that's more automated and is tied directly to our sales database.

Roger: Can you tell me your approximate per-unit cost for your current system?

C.J.: I don't have those figures at my fingertips, but I can arrange for you to get them. Do you think you could offer me something that's comparable?

Roger: I can't make a solid commitment until I see the numbers. But I can tell you that in general within the industry we're very competitive. I have some testimonials here from some of the big players in the industry, and as you can see, they're very happy with the services we provide. I wonder if you could tell me how you would like to be positioned vis-à-vis your competitors. That would give me a better idea of any advantages we could offer you.

It's an interesting change in Roger from the first conversation. At first glance it might seem that he's less confident, but if you look at what he's actually saying, you'll find an underlying confidence and professionalism that wasn't there the first time. Now he's not relying on sheer force of personality to bowl C.J. over. Instead, he's gone back to one of the basics of selling: the 80-20 rule.

Simply stated, the rule is that in any given sales call, you should be doing 20 percent of the talking, while your client should be doing 80 percent. I won't quibble about the numbers. Roger here may not be doing exactly 20 percent. But the point is that he's encouraging C.J. to talk, to tell him about her view of the industry and her insights into her business. That's because, at the end of the day, she's the one who's going to be running it, using the service that Roger is providing. And she's the one who'll be taking the financial risk.

Paradoxically, in my experience, people who act like Roger did in the first sales call do so not out of a surfeit of confidence but out of a lack of it. They're not entirely sure about the service they're selling, so they compensate by trying to push their way through with bluster and braggadocio. That may make them feel better, but in the long run it's not going to result in many sales. The more likely reaction is that the C.J.s of the industry are going to shut up their shutters and block out such sales calls. After all, no one likes being called an idiot.

HOW TO DIVIDE YOUR TIME IN A SALES CALL

Here's my general recommendation for a sales call. Let's assume the call takes an hour. The first 5 minutes should be spent on an introduction. Get to know the client, let her get to know you. (Of course, if you and the client already know one another, this is a good time to catch up on things, find out how you've been, and so on.)

The second 10 minutes should be spent on setting up the conversation. Give a broad, general outline of what you think you can do for the client and how it will benefit her.

The next 30 minutes should be spent asking questions. It doesn't have to be continuous; you don't have to make the client feel like she's wandered into a version of the Spanish Inquisition. But in general this part of the sales call should be spent trying to determine as much as possible about the client's business, the industry, the competition, and so forth. Remember, if you've done your research well, you should know the answers to some of the questions you're asking. The point, though, is to find out how the client sees these matters.

The next 10 minutes should be spent presenting your solutions to the problems the client has outlined. Why, you ask, only 10 minutes? Because the answers you're offering will grow organically out of the questions you've been asking in the middle 30 minutes.

Finally, the last 5 minutes of every sales call should be spent setting up the next visit. I can't overemphasize the importance of this stage. The whole object of your call is to keep the discussion going. Without the conversation, the sale is dead. As long as you're still talking, it's alive and the relationship is growing. And that's exactly what you want.

CONFIRMING YOUR CREDENTIALS

9

This story was told to me by a friend. I can vouch for its accuracy, amazing as it sounds.

My friend is in her forties but looks a bit younger. Still, she's got a few gray hairs here and there (I know she won't mind me saying this, because it's essential to understand the story that follows). She and a friend of about the same age went into a bar in a little town in New Jersey, where they happened to be staying.

Her friend ordered a beer, and Jessica (not her name) asked for a cocktail. This is where she started to get the sense that maybe they do things a little differently in Jersey.

"Can I see your ID?" the server asked.

Jessica was a little bemused. She hadn't been carded in, oh, probably 10 years. Still, she told herself, maybe it's some sort of house rule that they have to ask everyone who orders a drink for ID—though she did notice that her companion hadn't been carded. She dug into her purse and pulled out her wallet, then handed her driver's license to the waitress.

The girl—who, Jessica swears, couldn't have been more than 22 or 23—studied it for an eternity, then called her manager over. The manager studied the license with equal intensity, then turned to Jessica. "Do you have another piece of picture ID?" he asked.

Jessica hunted through her purse and told him no.

"I'm sorry," he said, "but we can't accept this ID."

Now Jessica was getting angry. "Why not?" she demanded.

"Because it's obviously fake," the manager told her. "Sorry, but no way were you born in 1962."

Part of Jessica wanted to thank him for the compliment, but the bigger part got angrier. "What are you talking about?" she shot back. "That's obviously my picture."

"Sorry," he replied. "I don't believe you. I'm going to have to ask you two to leave the bar."

Jessica couldn't believe it was actually happening until they were standing on the street outside the bar, shivering in the fall air.

CREDENTIALS GO DEEPER THAN APPEARANCES

When she told me this story some months later—in a bar, I might add, in which no one asked to see her license, much less questioned its validity—she'd gotten enough perspective on the story to see the humorous side of it. After all, how many women get in trouble at bars for looking too young? I advised her to take the compliment and be content with it.

However, one part of my brain stored up the story, and a year or two later I found myself repeating it to a group of salespeople. They thought it was funny, especially those who were from New Jersey, but I could tell they didn't quite get the point.

"Here's the takeaway," I told them. "Your credentials, those things that say you are who you say you are and you can do what you say you can do—those go much deeper than superficial appearances. Just because you tell your clients that you're a salesperson with two decades of experience doesn't mean they're going to accept you at face value. They may, they probably will, question you, and unless you can prove to their satisfaction that you know what you're talking about, they'll probably toss you out on your ear, figuratively or literally."

Nowhere is this idea truer than in selling services. I remarked a few chapters back on the challenge of selling something that the client can't prod or poke. Clients want, above all, to see results, but the results they'll see from the services you're selling may not show up for some time. They may even be *negative results*—for instance, you could argue that the real value of a good accounting firm lies in the fact that the client doesn't get audited.

Because of the abstract and occasionally negative quality of such products, clients want to see concrete proof that what they're buying is worthwhile. And the first place they turn for that proof is you, the salesperson. You're the most visible representation of the product—the service made flesh, so to speak. And at the end of the day, what you're selling on is your integrity, your promise that the service will do what you say it will do.

Now, no one is going to buy a service with that promise from someone he or she doesn't know on some level. In some cases, you'll build up a long relationship with clients, one in which they'll have an opportunity over many years to develop their confidence in you and will come to know you. You may even develop a friendship with them, although this presents its own challenges and perils.

But if you're selling to new clients, the absolute first thing they want to know is, who the hell are you, anyway? They don't necessarily mean this in a negative way, but it's a perfectly reasonable question. Why should I buy from someone I don't know? If selling is about relationships (and I can assure you after three and a half decades of doing it that it's *all* about relationships), how can I buy from someone whose credentials are questionable?

HOW TO BUILD TRUST

The instinct of most salespeople when confronted with this problem is to whip out a lengthy résumé. How long they've been selling. How many companies they've worked for. How many business degrees they've racked up. It's all interesting, but like Jessica's driver's license, it doesn't necessarily impress the audience. Because that's not what they want to know.

Customers—and I cannot repeat this too often in the course of this book—buy from you because they have a problem. What you are selling to them solves the problem. It doesn't matter if it's a physical product or a service to be performed at some point in the future once a contract is signed. If we start from this viewpoint, that a customer purchase is, for the customers, a potential solution to a problem, clearly what they want to know about you is, have you solved this problem for other people? And if so, how many times, how recently, and what were the consequences?

None of this should come as a surprise to you. In fact, the answers are in your résumé (or if they're not, they should be). The trick is to choose what to emphasize to the customer and how to present the information. It's a matter of packaging. It's possible, for instance, that had my friend Jessica said something when she handed over her driver's license to the waitress along the lines of, "Oh, I know that picture makes me seem older than I am, but isn't that just the way all driver's license photos come out?" that she might have gotten her drink.

I suggest that when you're selling to a new client, and especially if you're selling something like a service that's harder for the client to conceptualize, toward the beginning of your pitch you take a little time to talk about your results. Not about yourself but about what you've accomplished.

The results can be phrased in a way that doesn't make it seem as if you're presenting a towering paean of praise to yourself. Rather, it's a reasonable assumption on your part that the client will want to hear about cases similar to his and to understand the benefits that accrued to other of your customers when your company provided this service.

For instance, I might say something along the lines of, "During my career I've trained more than a half million salespeople. My estimate of the dollar amount this training has created is in the range of $500 million to $1 billion. So you can see here the value of the service I provide." After that, I spend a little time detailing how this service has worked in the past.

I don't gloss over my failures, especially if I think the client is likely to have heard of them. There's nothing that sinks your credentials faster than being dishonest or giving the appearance of dishonesty. But I don't dwell on them, either. My job is to create confidence in the client, confidence that I know what I'm doing and that I can deliver the results he's looking for. The more I can quantify that in dollars and cents, the better. This puts it in terms than anyone can understand and the client can make an equivalency to: If Steve's training resulted in W dollars' gain to this company with revenues of X, then my company, which has revenues of Y, will benefit to the amount of Z. Most of the time, clients will make that calculation themselves; every now and then you'll have to help them along a bit with some visual or mathematical aids.

It's quite possible that along the way your clients will ask personal questions about you. Don't be thrown by this; it's simply another way of establishing your credentials. Some types of clients (in my book *The 25 Toughest Sales Objections*, I outline four different types of clients) like to get to know you on a personal as well as a professional level. This is also just part of the process of establishing your credentials. You have to decide how much information you're comfortable revealing, but in most cases you can show quite a bit.

Just remember: you're the salesperson, and they're the clients. Don't let a friendship slide into a nonprofessional relationship. So long as you're selling to clients, the majority of your interactions with them must be on a professional rather than a personal level.

Credentials, as we've learned in this chapter, are an essential part of the selling process, and they're especially important when you're selling a service rather than a physical product. My last essential piece of advice on the subject is this: Once you establish your credentials, they're forever. They'll become one of your most important tools in picking up new clients and helping them to trust you. Get it right at the beginning, and it'll last a lifetime!

CLIENT CHALLENGE: "WHEN WILL I START TO SEE A DIFFERENCE?"

10

As I've indicated elsewhere in this book, to say nothing of the many other books I've written on sales and sales techniques, one of the basic mistakes you as a salesperson can make is to overpromise. This doesn't just mean exaggerating the benefits the client will realize from what you're selling; it means overstating the speed at which the client will start to see the benefits of your service or product.

In the case of a physical product, this is a somewhat easier proposition to control. If clients buy, for instance, a new, less expensive, and better material to manufacture their widgets, this change should be reflected almost immediately in their bottom line. They're spending less, making more, and, in theory, their customers are better satisfied. However, with services matters are often more abstract and harder to quantify. A service may take some time to reveal its superiority to an old system of doing things. An accounting firm can promise that its way of doing taxes will yield specific benefits, but it'll probably take a couple of years of data before the client can sit back and say, "Yes, it was a good thing I took that deal." This means that it's often tempting to overpromise what you can deliver.

SHIRKING THE RESPONSIBILITY TO ADDRESS A CLIENT'S PROBLEMS

Let's listen to a conversation between Sally, a salesperson for a firm of corporate tax accountants, and Mel, the CFO of a small business. Last year, Mel signed a three-year contract with Sally to use her tax services. Now it's June in the first year her company's done his taxes. Mel has called her, and he's not happy.

Mel: Sally, I have to tell you, I'm very, very concerned about our tax bill for this year.

Sally: Well, I understand that, but remember I told you that we couldn't guarantee that you'd start to see your bill decline immediately.

Mel: Now, wait a minute! That's almost exactly what you did say! You told me when we negotiated this agreement last November that you'd guarantee that our tax bill for the next three years would see a decline each year by a minimum of 5 percent.

Sally: Is that written into the contract?

Mel: No, but I remember you saying that when we were discussing it.

Sally: Well, bottom line, Mel, I don't think it's in the contract. You should know that it's hard to guarantee anything these days in regard to taxes—especially with a new bill having gone through Congress and changes in the state code.

Mel: But this throws off my budgeting for next year. I'm being hit with almost $20,000 in additional taxes.

Sally: Look, I think that's probably not that bad. I can guarantee that at the end of the three-year period that the contract has to run, you'll see that your tax bill will, on average, have dropped by around 5 percent a year.

Mel: Sally, this is completely unacceptable! What are you going to do about it?

Sally: Really, there's nothing I can do about it. It's the federal government and the state government. What're you going to do? This is why we prefer to keep the contract itself a bit easy on these points.

Mel: All right. Bottom line: when am I going to see the benefits you promised me from this deal?

Sally: As I said earlier, at the end of the three years you should see an overall decline in your tax bill. In total, you'll save around 15 percent, which means you're seeing a decline of about 5 percent a year—which is what I promised you. I really don't see what you're so upset about.

Admittedly this is a made-up conversation, so I've exaggerated a bit—but not very much. In my time as a sales trainer, I've heard salespeople on the phone with clients take a tone not much less abrasive than the one adopted by Sally. There are several reasons for this:

1. Sally really has no respect for Mel. Having signed the deal, she's ceased to feel any real responsibility for it. You can feel this coming through in her responses; her real goal in the conversation is to get Mel off the phone so she can get back to contacting other leads who are likely to turn into sales.

2. Sally absolves herself of any ability to fix the problem. As she so eloquently puts it, "There's nothing I can do about

it." If I had my way, that sentence would be surgically re-moved from the vocabularies of salespeople everywhere. It's about the worst thing you can say when a client in distress calls you.

Whenever you say something like this, you're effectively telling the client, "Sorry, you're not important to me and I won't stir a finger to fix whatever's bothering you." Now, it may be true that the client's demands are unreasonable and difficult, but that doesn't ever excuse you from trying your best to address them. It's the client who's effectively paying your commission—never forget that.

3. Sally focuses on legalisms and the letter of the contract rather than the spirit. I admit that in this case Mel is to some extent to blame for not having read the final agree-ment carefully, but that doesn't minimize what amounts to Sally's basic dishonesty. She is admitting, implicitly, that she told Mel one thing during negotiations and wrote some-thing else into the final contract. That should never, ever be the case. The contract should be a legal record of the dis-cussions and agreements you and the client had. Anything outside of that is going to come back to bite you.

4. Sally is trying to minimize the damage that's been done to the client as a result of her sale, which is something no one wants to hear. Whatever else your clients are looking for, I absolutely guarantee you that one thing they don't enjoy is being told that their concerns aren't important. That im-plies they don't understand their own business. It's insulting and shockingly disrespectful on Sally's part.

5. Here's the most important point regarding selling services: The client needs to understand right up front what guar-antees you're making and when they will appear. If Sally's

firm believed that on average the client would see a reduction of 5 percent a year in his tax bill over the three years of the contact, well, that's a perfectly quantifiable, defensible benefit. But Sally should have said that. What she said instead was something quite different: She guaranteed Mel a reduction in his first year's tax bill of 5 percent, something her company can't stand behind.

In short, Sally's reaction to Mel's anger is a combination of mealymouthed weaseling and shirking responsibility. Of course, she's signed a three-year contract with his company, probably for a hefty fee. But it's all but guaranteed that he'll never work with her again.

THE CUSTOMER-CENTRIC RESPONSE

Now let's imagine how that phone call might have gone if Sally were truly a customer-centric salesperson.

Mel: Sally, I have to tell you, I'm very, very concerned about our tax bill for this year.

Sally: I'm sorry, Mel. Why don't you tell me about your concerns?

Mel: Well, the chief one is that we're not seeing nearly the tax benefits from your accounting service that I expected.

Sally: I see. What sort of number could you attach to the tax benefits you were expecting?

Mel: I projected in our budget about $20,000 less in taxes than we'll be paying.

Sally: That is a big number. I can understand your concern. I don't have your records here in front of me, but let me pull them and talk to the people who worked them up. I'll get back to you at 10 a.m. tomorrow morning. Is that acceptable?

Mel: Yes, that's fine.

Okay, let's stop here a moment. What did Sally do that was different?

1. She apologized for the client's problem. Even though it's not yet clear if the problem was actually caused by Sally's company, she knows that Mel wants to hear some sympathy and a willingness by Sally to take ownership of the problem.

2. She asked for more information. Rather than immediately back up into a defensive posture, she tries to get some facts and figures about what's going on.

3. Rather than make a summary judgment and just stand on the letter of the contract, Sally indicates that she's going to get additional information from the people who prepared the return for Mel's company.

4. She makes an appointment to discuss things with Mel again, and she's specific as to a date and time. This is huge. It's very tempting to say something like, "Well, this could take a while, so I'll get back to you as soon as I can." Don't do that! From the client's standpoint you're just stalling; even if Sally doesn't have an answer by 10 a.m. the following morning, she should call Mel back and tell him that and ask for a bit more time. That way Mel knows she's working on the problem.

Now let's jump ahead to the 10 a.m. phone call.

Sally: Mel, I spoke to the people who prepared your returns. I've also looked at the terms of our contract to see what guarantees we made to you. And I've spoken to my supervisor to find out what our options are.

Mel: I see. So what's the story?

Sally: The figures on your return are based on the current tax code, including all the deductions we feel you can reasonably take. At the time you and I last spoke, you may remember that there was a lot of speculation that the tax code would be revised to allow a greater number of deductions for small businesses. However, as you know, that revision did not occur. Our contract states that we will provide tax returns based on the current tax code, which is what we did.

Mel: Well, that still messes up this year's budget plans for me.

Sally: I know how you feel. Let me ask you this—would you have some time next week to set aside to work on this problem? Say about four or five hours?

Mel: Sure. This is a big problem for me. I'll spend as much time on it as I have to.

Sally: That's great. Here's what we can do. We can request from the government an extension on filing taxes. We'll do that on your behalf; all you have to do is sign the paperwork when we send it over. Then next week the accountant we've assigned to you, John Moore, will call you and go over your return, line by line, so we can determine if there are any further deductions you can take. I can't guarantee anything, of course, to a specific dollar amount, but I can tell you that when we've done this in the past, we've found that there are often deductions that have been overlooked and that can result in a substantial savings. Does that sound like a workable plan?

Mel: Yes, that sounds great.

Sally: Wonderful. I'll ask John to get in touch with you later today, and as soon as we're off this phone call I'll send you an e-mail with his contact information so you can follow up with him. Meanwhile, we'll draw up the papers for the extension and fax them to you. They should reach you this afternoon.

Mel: Good.

Sally: One more thing. Just to make sure that everything goes okay, let's set up another time for you and me to speak after you've worked with John Moore. Could we say a week from today at 10 a.m.?

Mel: Great. I'll mark it in my calendar. Thanks for your help.

Sally: No problem. I'm happy we could help you.

Now we've gotten someplace. Sally has put a potential solution in place, with a timeline about when the different stages are going to happen. She's set up a time and date for follow-up. Notice also that she hasn't guaranteed anything—Mel's tax bill will still probably be higher than he'd like. But at least he's not going to blame Sally and her company for it.

THE BASICS OF GOOD COMMUNICATION

11

As I've remarked in a couple of my other books on sales, I'm a fan of the Marx Brothers. Their insane routines turned the staid and formulaic comedy of the 1930s on its head. Each of them created a distinctly different character, and by playing these characters rather than the situation, they created timeless gems of comic genius.

Among their most hilarious routines are the exchanges between Groucho and any hapless bystander foolish enough to get in his way. Consider this conversation between the mustached comedian and a ship's captain from *Monkey Business*:

Groucho: I want to register a complaint.

Captain: Why, what's the matter?

Groucho: Matter enough! Do you know who sneaked into my stateroom at three o'clock this morning?

Captain: Who did that?

Groucho: Nobody. And that's my complaint. I'm young. I want gaiety, laughter, ha-cha-cha! I wanna dance! I wanna dance till the cows come home.

Aside from the strangeness of Groucho complaining that he *wasn't* disturbed at three in the morning, what should strike you about this exchange (once you've stopped laughing) is that Groucho and the captain aren't really having a conversation. Each of them is talking, but their remarks are just flying by one another. Groucho's sentences, as critic Joe Adamson remarked, "lose their way, fail to accomplish what they set out to accomplish and are proud of it." The captain, to give him credit, tries to engage but is outtalked and outmaneuvered at every turn. Finally, in despair, he turns to threats. "One more word out of you," he snarls, "and I'll put you in irons!"

"You can't do it with irons," Groucho blithely replies. "It's a mashie shot. It's a mashie shot if the wind's against you, and if the wind isn't, I am!"

The captain retires, defeated.

All of this is well and good in the movie theater or on late-night television. But, as I can tell you from bitter experience, it's a lot more serious when it occurs in the realm of sales.

In fact, one of the main problems I find with sales when I listen to salespeople talk about their experiences in the field is that too often salespeople and clients don't talk to one another, they talk at each other. Like Groucho and the captain, their words fly by one another and fail to connect.

COMMUNICATING, NOT JUST TALKING

This tendency is particularly pronounced when salespeople are selling services rather than physical products. I suspect this is because when salespeople are talking about something that seems abstract, they find it easier to start engaging in windy generalities. These sorts of statements may sound impressive at first, but after a while they're just a lot of hot air.

Communication is, I fear, becoming something of a lost art these days, thanks partly to the Internet. People seem to think that e-mail gives them license for sloppy language, thought, and communication. I'm constantly shocked to receive e-mails that pay no attention at all to the rules of punctuation or spelling. Not surprisingly, I usually have a hard time figuring out what the senders of these e-mails really want. The untidiness of their communication reflects the sloppiness of their thinking. And, sadly, the Internet encourages this sort of thing because it focuses on speed rather than clarity.

With this in mind, I've set out to decide on a set of rules for effective communication. I'm putting them in this book because I think that especially when you're selling services, it's essential to make sure the client knows exactly what you're talking about. Any lack of clarity, any imprecision and carelessness about communication will come up in one of two places: the contract and follow-up. More on this in a little bit. For now, here are the Schiffman Rules of Effective Communication:

1. Decide beforehand on the three or four most important points you want to make. Plan the discussion in your mind before having it and make sure you prioritize your most essential messages. That way you're less likely to become distracted by all the fascinating side avenues that the conversation can wander down.

2. Try to look at the issues from the client's point of view and anticipate his responses. Sometimes it's useful to actually have the conversation beforehand, playing both roles. (Be sure to do this when no one else is around. If you attract the attention of your wife, she's likely to think you've gone around the bend.) Remember that the client's views are going to play an equal role in the

discussion with your own, and you must respond to them and not push them aside.

3. Begin the discussion by stating the main points you hope to make and that you want to conclude with. You don't need to be repetitious (which is boring). But keep in mind the basic formula for communication: tell them what you're going to tell them; tell it to them; and tell them what you've told them.

4. Combine responsiveness with a firm direction. This is one of the biggest mistakes I see young salespeople make: they're so anxious not to step on the client's toes that they let her or him take over the meeting and lead it in directions it shouldn't go. If clients bring up a point they want to discuss, you must respond, but don't let it pull you off message. Come back, in your mind, to those most important points you set as your mental agenda for the meeting.

5. Remember the value of summary. At the end of the meeting, reiterate what you've discussed, what you've agreed on, and what's left to talk about at your next meeting. That'll help set the agenda for your next encounter, and it will confirm to everyone what's been said. As soon as possible after the meeting, send a follow-up e-mail, going over these points. I can't overemphasize the value of developing a paper trail like this. It will be of huge importance when you come to draw up the contract and can refer back to it in support of specific clauses.

Sticking to these points will help you keep your meetings focused and will prevent the Groucho Marxes of the sales world from talking rings around you. In respect to selling a service, it also allows you to keep the discussion grounded.

The clients will, for the most part, appreciate this. After all, their time is valuable too, and they don't want to waste it in pointless rambling. If you sense that a meeting is going astray, take a quick mental review of your agenda items and say something to get it back on track.

FOCUSING ON THE POSITIVES

A couple of other points are worth keeping in mind in the matter of developing and maintaining effective communication skills:

1. You don't need to settle everything in one meeting. There are exceptions to this, of course, but in general you shouldn't feel compelled to work out every detail in your first meeting with the client. It may well be that there are questions you have to talk over with your boss, issues the client has to discuss with his bosses, and so on. Try not to feel rushed, and do what you need to do in order to slow down the meeting to a reasonable pace.

2. If there's an issue that's becoming a significant point of contention, sometimes the best thing to do is put it aside for a while. Focus on the smaller points on which you can find agreement. Keep the tone of the meeting positive. Often the bigger issues will start to resolve themselves as you solve the smaller ones.

3. Remember that everyone wants this to work. I'm saddened by the number of times I've had to remind salespeople of this basic axiom. Both you and the client want an agreement. That's why you're talking. If you didn't, you wouldn't be in the same room together. So if you sense you're drifting apart, remind the client of the benefits of what you're selling and refocus your collective energies on the deal. Stress the positives rather than the negatives.

The biggest threat to good communication, in my experience, is ego. Some salespeople (and other people from all walks of life) are so intent on making their point, pushing themselves forward, making sure that everyone knows it's about me that they miss the bigger picture. You get big in sales by making the sale. There's no reason to push yourself forward every chance you get; there'll be time enough for everyone to recognize what a great job you've done after the sale is finished and you're back in the office celebrating.

A final point about good communication: it's essential that you build your sales vocabulary. I'm surprised, in a way, that more salespeople don't understand this point. Everyone in a particular industry talks a special language. They exchange comments in a kind of shorthand that other people don't necessarily understand. If you're going to sell in an industry, it's absolutely crucial that you know what words, nicknames, and acronyms are used to describe the industry's components. Otherwise, you sound like an outsider—and you are one. Imagine coming into a new business—for example, sales—and not knowing terms such as *cold calling, clients, point of sale,* and *discount.* If anyone tried talking to you while showing ignorance of those things, you'd dismiss him or her out of hand, wouldn't you? Why do you think your clients are any different? They want to make sure you're one of them, part of the educated few who understand how their industry works. Then they'll talk to you about doing a deal. Not before.

I believe that nine-tenths of communication is confidence. You've got to believe in what you're saying and what you're selling in order to put the sale across. But it's also got to be true—you can't sell something that's false or fake. That's the other part of communication. It's about putting into words something you believe is true. That doesn't always make it easier. But at least it makes it possible.

As Groucho would say, "You bet your life!"

CLIENT CHALLENGE: "I DON'T UNDERSTAND WHAT YOU'RE SAYING"

12

Some of you reading this book (I hope, most of you) probably read *Alice in Wonderland* when you were younger. You may even have read its companion piece, *Alice Through the Looking-Glass*. If you're familiar with the latter, you might recall Alice's conversation with Humpty Dumpty on the subject of words:

> "I don't know what you mean by 'glory,'" Alice said.

> Humpty Dumpty smiled contemptuously. "Of course you don't—till I tell you. I meant, 'There's a nice knock-down argument for you!'"

> "But 'glory' doesn't mean 'a nice knock-down argument,'" Alice objected.

> "When I use a word," Humpty Dumpty said in rather a scornful tone, "it means just what I choose it to mean—neither more or less."

> "The question is," said Alice, "whether you *can* make words mean so many different things."

"The question is," said Humpty Dumpty, "which is to be master—that's all."

I quote this because I think it's an excellent illustration of how and why communication so often goes astray. "The greatest myth of communication," said George Bernard Shaw, "is the illusion that it has been accomplished." I think old GBS knew a thing or two—as did Humpty Dumpty.

To put things in a nutshell, too often when two people are speaking to each other, there's a miscommunication because they're thinking of words in two different ways. Consider the following conversation between Jeremy, a salesperson for a security services firm, and David, a small business owner.

David: Jeremy, when we spoke last month and I signed up with you guys, you told me that you provided a comprehensive package of services.

Jeremy: That's right. We do.

David: Well, I have to tell you that I'm pretty underimpressed so far with the service you're providing.

Jeremy: Why's that? What's wrong?

David: Well, you know we had an attempted break-in last week.

Jeremy: Yes, I saw the report on it. Everything okay?

David: No. No, it's not okay. The thieves didn't get anything, thank goodness, but they jimmied the lock on our back door and cracked the frame.

Jeremy: But nothing was taken, right? The alarm went off just like it's supposed to, and one of our operators called you and said you told her to call the police.

David: Yes, yes, that was fine. The police showed up very promptly, and they've been very helpful.

Jeremy: So what's the problem?

David: What are you going to do about my broken lock and cracked doorframe?

Jeremy: Oh, that's your responsibility.

David: But when you said "comprehensive package—"

Jeremy: Look, we did what we had to do under the contract, okay? We installed the alarm system, and our operator did her job. What more did you expect?

David: I expected someone from your company to come out and inspect the damage and contact a contractor about fixing it. As it is, I can't open until it's fixed, and I've had to spend the last night on the premises to make sure we didn't have any more problems.

Jeremy: Well, that's all in the contract.

David: I'm not going to renew my contract with you people again. And you can be sure that none of the other businesses in this area will either.

Oh, dear. Not only has Jeremy's miscommunication cost him a customer, but he's alienated David to the point that David's going to cost him more business by telling everyone he knows not to use Jeremy's security firm.

Like Alice's conversation with Humpty Dumpty, the problem lies in trying to make a word mean too many things. In this case, the word is comprehensive. I don't like that word, as a general rule, precisely for this reason. It's too open to misunderstanding, both by the salesperson and by the client. In this case, David thought *comprehensive* included much more than it did.

You can argue, of course, that David's at fault for not having read his contract closely. But that doesn't really fix the problem. Jeremy should have made sure that David knew exactly what services were included in the package and how they would be administered.

And look at Jeremy's attitude throughout the call. It's disinterested, bordering on rudeness. A break-in is a very traumatic event for a small business owner. It's like having your home burglarized. But Jeremy shows no sympathy and barely an interest. Instead, he immediately sets himself up as an adversary, standing on the letter of the contract, challenging David. The result is exactly what you'd expect: David feels threatened and betrayed.

TAKE RESPONSIBILITY FOR ANY MISUNDERSTANDINGS

I've said elsewhere that the contract stage of negotiations is where all ambiguities and questions are pushed into the open. That assumes, of course, that the salesperson is conscientious about going through the contract with the client and that the client is paying careful attention. But you do have cases—and this seems to be one of them—where one or both parties fall down on this responsibility. Under such circumstances it is the primary responsibility of the salesperson to pick up the pieces and fix the problem. Let me repeat that to be very clear: It's your responsibility to fix the problems that result from miscommunication. If you push it back on your client, you won't have a client very long.

So what to do in this case?

Well, let's assume that at the contract stage, neither Jeremy nor David was thinking too clearly and David signed up for a "comprehensive" security package without a real understanding of what that entailed. Now imagine how the conversation might go if Jeremy got on the ball.

David: Jeremy, when we spoke last month and I signed up with you guys, you told me that you provided a comprehensive package of services. That's what I signed up for.

Jeremy: That's right, David. Are you displeased with some aspect of the package?

David: Damn right. You know we had a break-in a couple of nights ago at the store.

Jeremy: Yes, I heard about it from the operator who handled the alarm call. I'm very sorry to hear it. Are you okay?

David: Yeah, sure. I'm just glad that the alarm went off and scared away the burglars.

Jeremy: Hold on just a second. I'm pulling up my logbook for that night. Yes, we show that the alarm went off at 2:15 a.m. and the operator called you 30 seconds after receiving notification of the alarm. The police arrived at the scene at 2:29.

David: That sounds right.

Jeremy: Well, these things are always difficult, but I'm glad the system functioned the way it's supposed to. Now, what aspect of what happened is concerning you?

David: Well, I'll tell you. When the thieves tried to break in, they jimmied the lock and cracked the doorframe, so it's going to have to be replaced.

Jeremy: I see.

David: But nobody from your company has contacted me about coming out and doing a replacement. I've had to spend the last two nights in the store to make sure we don't have any more break-ins.

Jeremy: I'm very sorry you had to do that. Let's take a look at your contract, David. Do you have a copy handy?

David: Yeah. I'm pulling it up.

Jeremy: Great. Just go to page 6 and let's go over the list of services provided. I'm looking down it, and I don't see anything about replacing damaged property. Is that what you're seeing?

David: Yeah, no, I think you're right. So that's not included in this package? I wish I'd known that at the time I signed up for it.

Jeremy: I take full responsibility for not going over this section in detail with you at the time we signed, David. I fell down on the job there. But let's figure out your immediate problem. You've got to get that doorframe and lock fixed right away.

David: Yeah.

Jeremy: David, how about if I make some phone calls to repair people in your area? I'll get back to you with a list of their estimates, and you can pick the one you prefer. Then let me know, and I'll arrange for them to come out and take care of the problem right away. We can't cover the cost, unfortunately, but we can certainly help you out with the details of arranging for the work to be done.

David: That'd be great if you could do that. I appreciate it.

Jeremy: No problem. I'll have that list for you in about a half hour or so. Why don't we talk again this afternoon at 2 p.m., and you can let me know who you want to use to do the work.

David: Okay.

All right, now things are going better. I'd argue that it would have been best if Jeremy had called David as soon as he received notice of the break-in. But even without that, he's still showing interest and concern in his client's problem. By suggesting that they go over the relevant contract clause together, he's making the investigation a cooperative rather than a competitive activity.

And although he makes clear that his security company can't cover the costs of the lock and doorframe, he's going beyond customer expectations in offering to handle setting up the job.

MAKE SURE YOUR COMMUNICATION IS CLEAR

I chose this particular example because it's very clear-cut. Other issues having to do with language are potentially much more complicated. One of the things that contributes to this confusion is the Internet, which has blurred the line between public and private property in many cases. In order to avoid confusion and argument over words, I suggest the following guidelines:

1. In your discussions with the client, be very cautious with words such as *absolute, forever, always, permanent, guarantee,* and *promise.* These are sometimes good words to use, but they have significant implications that can get you into trouble down the road.

2. It's always better to underpromise and overdeliver. Be conservative in your estimates of what your service can do—not so conservative, of course, that you talk the client out of doing the deal, but not overpromising, either. Then, when possible, call attention to instances where you've been able to exceed expectations.

3. At the end of a complex negotiating session, give a brief oral summary of what you've agreed to. Follow it up with a written summary in the form of an e-mail. This is very important for making sure everyone is on the same page and knows what he or she's agreed to.

4. Set aside enough time for a thorough review of the contract by both you and the client.

5. Make sure the client has read—really read—the contract and understood it. Some salespeople think they're slick for slipping a contract past a client, barely giving him time to glance at the terms. That's a losing game. All those salespeople are doing is creating a pool of clients who'll be very angry in the future and do serious harm to the reputation of the sales company. If the client has read and understood the contract, there's much less room for later misunderstandings.

6. Because a service's benefits are generally realized over time, in your contacts with the client provide a constant update and running total of the benefits your service is generating. That way there's less chance of the client calling up to complain that it's been six months and he's yet to see any real change in his numbers.

STYLES OF COMMUNICATING

Recently I was talking to a colleague of mine, someone who's spent almost as long as I have in the field of sales and sales training. Both of us, in other words, are seasoned professionals with a lot of experience under our belts. As a result, we have a good deal to talk about, and we're rarely surprised by one another's anecdotes.

On this occasion, though, I have to say that my friend told me a story that had me shaking my head in wonder.

He'd been working to sign a new client, a firm that makes some of the internal gadgets that are used in the pumps at service stations. The company was small, with about 100 employees, and it had been involved in this business for about 40 years. My colleague was pitching a training session for the company's four-person sales force—not a huge contract, of course, but given that he'd done careful research on the company and studied its competition, its past sales and revenue numbers, and its suppliers and their customers, he figured this one was in the bag. He'd budgeted 45 minutes for the sales call; at the end of that time he had a 30-minute drive to his next call and 40 minutes planned for lunch.

When he got to the company, everything seemed fine. The owner (son of the company's founder) was pleasant and clearly was enthusiastic about his company's prospects. The two sat down in the owner's office, and my colleague dug into his computer's files for the PowerPoint slides he'd prepared.

What he wasn't ready for was, before he even got a chance to start, the owner sitting back in his chair and saying, "Roger, what do you think of the situation in Venezuela?"

He might as well have asked Roger about the latest research into quantum mechanics. Roger flailed around for a moment and pulled out some nondescript reply. The owner shook his head slightly and said, "D'you think Chavez is really sick?" (Hugo Chavez, the president of Venezuela, had recently traveled to Cuba for a highly publicized operation.)

Roger couldn't think of an answer that was going to get him anywhere. "Maybe," he said. "I don't know." He clicked on his first slide and began, "Now, as you can see here—"

The owner interrupted again with a question about the Middle East. What did Roger think about the rising tensions between the United States and Iran?

Roger was bewildered. These were interesting questions if you were involved in geopolitics, but he was talking about training a sales force. He fumbled through another answer. And . . .

Just like that, the call was over.

Roger realized afterward, of course, what you may have already figured out: the business of petroleum in the United States is very dependent on international events. A political change in Venezuela or war between America and Iran could drastically affect the price of oil and with it gas prices at the pump. Higher gas prices meant consumers would buy less gas. Lower gas sales meant less business for a company that made gas pumps. It was that simple. What the owner wanted to know was how much these connections were in the forefront of Roger's mind.

As I say, Roger had figured this out almost before he was out of the building. What threw him was not so much the substance of what the owner was communicating to him—it was the style. The fact that these questions were being tossed at him without any sort of warning made him feel as if he was swinging blind, trying to hit one of them without any idea of where it would go.

HOW YOU COMMUNICATE IS AS IMPORTANT AS WHAT YOU COMMUNICATE

The whole experience illustrates a basic point about selling: Often what is being communicated takes a backseat, at least temporarily, to how it's being communicated. And misinterpreting a communication style can be disastrous.

The incident reminded me of something from my own past when I was in the trenches as a day-to-day salesperson. At one point early in my career, I'd begun working for a new boss. He asked to meet with all the salespeople in the organization, and we lined up 15-minute meetings with him, one after the other. When my turn came, I was prepared to explain to him what I did, how I did it, and what value I was bringing to the organization—all good, solid information, backed up by facts and figures.

But instead, he started off the meeting by asking about my family life. From there, he segued into a discussion about hobbies, vacation plans, what sort of music I enjoyed, and who I'd worked for in the past. In no time at all, my 15 minutes was up. I hadn't had a chance to present any of my information to him, and he didn't show much interest in giving me extra time to do so. Instead, he thanked me politely and asked his admin to send in the next person in line.

Talking to my fellow salespeople afterward, all of whom had had similar experiences, we finally figured out that this was the boss's way of communicating. Rather than take a straightforward approach, which we were all used to, he preferred to approach matters indirectly, usually by focusing on a personal issue.

Personally, I find this method uncomfortable, and I'm not a fan of it. But it helped me to understand it when I encountered it from my boss—and it's stood me in good stead in later years when I've come across it again.

Why talk about this in a book that's concerned with selling services? Because when you're selling something that to many people seems abstract and ethereal, understanding both your own communication style and that of the person you're talking to can take on added importance.

THREE MAIN COMMUNICATION STYLES

Styles of communication are very much tailored to the individual doing the communicating, and there are as many styles as there are people. That said, I think there are three big styles that I've encountered over the years: aggressive, passive, and interactive.

AGGRESSIVE AND PASSIVE COMMUNICATORS

Aggressive communicators start from the premise that they know everything and you know nothing. They believe words are power, and they're perfectly willing to use them to beat you down and force you into retreat. To an aggressive communicator, communication is not a two-way street; instead, it's a battlefield, on which there can only be one victor.

Not surprisingly, an aggressive communicator will start by challenging you on your facts, your opinions, and your premises. If you tell him that what you're selling will improve his numbers by up to 20 percent, he'll demand that you show proof of that and then discount the proof as being flawed and indecisive. He'll argue with you at every stage of your presentation and perhaps beyond that. Moreover, he has no compunction about allowing the discussion to become personal. If he sees that descending to personalities pushes your buttons and is likely to make you retreat and offer concessions, well, that's the way he's going to go.

I don't personally like this style of communication, but I'd be the last person to say that it doesn't often work. The aggressive communicator will watch you like a hawk, sizing you up for weaknesses, and then attack.

The second style of communication you'll see a lot is passive. This is the style used by my former boss, whom I described to you in the passage above. Passive communicators are less about passing along information than they are about getting you to make the connections. From their standpoint, this has two advantages:

1. They control just how much information you receive.

2. They don't have to take responsibility for the conclusions you draw from that information.

This sort of communication can be particularly frustrating for salespeople trained in the Schiffman School of Sales, because as you know I advocate asking questions as the most basic part of a sales call. With a passive communicator, getting answers to those questions can feel like trying to dig coal with a toothpick—you just don't seem to be getting anywhere, but getting mad at the coal doesn't get you anywhere, either.

When you're on the receiving end of either the aggressive or the passive schools of communication, the temptation is to retaliate in kind. When a client starts yelling at you, too often you want to yell back. If a client seems to want to talk about anything other than your sales pitch, it's easy to go along with him.

However, I recommend strongly that you resist that temptation.

Yelling at an aggressive communicator will, mostly, get you nowhere and simply escalate the argument until there's a loud pop and fragments of your sales call are scattered all over the conference room. (There's an exception to every rule, though. On rare occasions, when you're being bullied by an aggressive communicator, pushing back can make the person back off. You've got to carefully gauge such situations and play them by ear.) Rather than yelling, my usual approach is to try to calm things down while holding firm to my offer. In the case of a passive communicator, I try to hone my questions to be more and more specific, so there's as little wiggle room as possible. At the same time, I resolutely refuse to get off track.

INTERACTIVE COMMUNICATORS

The third communication style is interactive. This is the one you'll probably feel most comfortable with, since it's best adapted to a question-based sales call. People who use this style of communication see discussion as a back-and-forth exchange of ideas and information. They want your opinion, but at the same time, they have no inhibition about giving you theirs. They want to know what you know. But they're not information hoarders (something characteristic of passive communicators).

The one point of caution I'd throw up here is this: Interactive communicators don't like to feel that you're not playing along with them. If you're reluctant to offer your opinions or data, talking to someone such as this can become a nightmare.

Communication is very much a matter of thinking quickly on your feet. When you're dealing with new clients, you're walking into a lot of unknowns, and one of the biggest ones is the style of your prospective partner. It's much easier, of course, when you're dealing with long-established clients; preparing for those sales calls, you'll know whether you'll be coming back to the office with your ears ringing from the client's shouting, exasperated with trying to get the client to tell you anything, or cheerful after a long, productive exchange about the industry, the business, and the service you're offering.

CLIENT CHALLENGE: "WE'RE TALKING PAST EACH OTHER"

14

In a previous chapter I spoke about the challenges that arise when you and the client mean different things even when you're speaking the same words. Here I want to consider another case of miscommunication: When you and the client are simply talking past one another. You might as well be in two different rooms having a conversation with someone else.

Some time ago, my wife and I went to see the musical *Les Misérables*. It was a wonderful experience. The show, which has been playing on Broadway for decades, was moving and uplifting to both of us. We found deeply compelling moments in the story of the hero, Jean Valjean, who spends his whole life atoning for his one act of weakness, pursued by his implacable enemy, Inspector Javert. In the end, of course, it's Javert who comes across as the villain of the piece because he's pitiless even in the face of Valjean's obvious saintly qualities. When Javert is confronted with the evidence of Valjean's mercy toward him (Valjean could have turned him over to the rebellious French students for summary justice and doesn't), he's unable to stand this contradiction in his principles. Despairing, he throws himself from a bridge into the flood-swollen Seine River and drowns.

Early in the show, there's a key scene in which Valjean and Javert confront one another at the deathbed of Fantine, a factory girl whom Valjean has taken under his wing. Javert, having finally cornered his former prisoner (or so he thinks), savors his triumph over Valjean. The latter pleads for a little time to rescue Fantine's daughter, to whom he's pledged his protection, from her situation as a virtual slave to the villainous Thénardiers.

"Valjean, at last, we see each other plain," shouts Javert. Valjean appeals for a moment of mercy, but Javert is beyond such reproaches.

"You must think me mad. A man like you can never change, a man such as you," Valjean replies, singing over Javert's countering lyrics, while Javert cries back his answer—there can be no exceptions, no pardons for men such as Valjean who have stepped beyond the law.

What struck me as I listened to this magnificent duet was that Valjean and Javert are speaking (or singing, if you like) to one another, but they aren't communicating. In fact, the very act of their speaking to one another makes their communication impossible. It further struck me that I've heard a lot of salespeople fall into this trap.

Let's listen in on a conversation between Alan, a salesperson, and Rachel, the buyer for a midlevel company. Alan is pitching a new fulfillment system to Rachel.

Alan: The thing we're most proud of in our new fulfillment system is that the time from when the order is received in the warehouse to the point when it leaves has been reduced to 45 minutes. I think you'll find that this is more than competitive.

Rachel: What's the level of quality control here? Because with our previous fulfillment system—

Alan: A lot of the time we save here is because we've automated the pick system, at least as much as we can.

Rachel: Most of the mistakes we find in the system are easily correctable, but there's a level of error that we find unacceptable.

Alan: We also find that we can improve our system by integrating clients into our warehouse structure. Your products will be housed at depots in the Midwest, Southwest, West Coast, and Northeast.

Rachel: The biggest concern I have is that errors in fulfillment are costing us a substantial amount not just to correct them but in terms of customer goodwill.

Alan: With the dedicated staff at these depots, we find that we can—

Rachel: Alan?

Alan: Yes?

Rachel: Have you actually been listening to anything I've said? I get the impression that you don't care about my concerns at all.

Alan: No, you're wrong about that.

Rachel: Really? Then how are you going to address the issues I raised about quality control?

Alan: I'm sorry. Could you restate your concerns again? I don't think you fully outlined them before.

Rachel: No, I think we're done. Thanks for your time.

And that's it. Alan's out the door, the deal is blown, and Rachel is silently vowing never to do business with him again. What a complete waste of everyone's time and energy.

Did anything strike you in reading through this? Yes, me too. Rachel and Alan were having two entirely different conversations. It's not *Les Miz*, but like Valjean and Javert, they weren't communicating with one another. Neither was listening to the other, neither cared what the other had to say, and neither was going to find any measure of satisfaction in a resolution.

Although that's the case, I want to stress that the onus on solving the problem lies entirely with Alan. He's the one who initiated the meeting. He's the one with something to sell. Most important, from my standpoint, he's the one who should know better. As a result, he's ticking off Rachel by ignoring her and flying along on his own wavelength.

FOCUS ON YOUR MUTUAL GOAL: SOLVING THE CLIENT'S PROBLEM

No one ever wants to feel extraneous to a conversation. I can tell you this from painful experience. At a party I attended not too long ago, I was standing with several other people who began to have an intensive discussion about the prospects of a New York sports team (out of respect, I refrain from specifying which one). I listened to the conversation, trying to feel involved, and finally I was struck by the fact that I'd been moved outside the magic circle. Now I was an outsider, looking in, trying to understand terms, grasping at meanings, and feeling . . . excluded.

It was very unpleasant, I can tell you. I moved away from the group, downed another drink, and looked for my overcoat. I don't like feeling on the outside. Neither does Rachel. Neither does any client. So that's your first lesson from this: Don't exclude the client.

The second point is a little less obvious but no less important. You make progress with clients by listening to them. I've already explained my principles of active listening. But in addition, you have to respond directly to their statements, to engage them in conversation, to let them direct where the discussion is going to go. The advantage of doing this is twofold: First, you find out a lot of valuable information that will be of great use to you in the sales call. Second, you find out what's important to the client. And what's important to the client should be important to you.

The third lesson is a bit more complicated. You have to go where the client wants to go. But at the same time, you can't put the client entirely in charge of the conversation. Instead, by active listening and some skillful footwork, you have to focus the discussion on what's important both to you and to the client—solving her problem.

COMMUNICATION STARTS WITH ACTIVE LISTENING

With this in mind, let's rerun that conversation, and this time let's let Rachel and Alan communicate instead of talking past one another.

Alan: The thing we're most proud of in our new fulfillment system is that the time from when the order is received in the warehouse to the point when it leaves has been reduced to 45 minutes. I think you'll find that this is more than competitive.

Rachel: What's the level of quality control here? Because with our previous fulfillment system we found that our partner was more focused on speed of fulfillment rather than actually getting the orders right.

Alan: That's an interesting point. Was this something consistent from the time you installed the system?

Rachel: Not at first, no. It seemed to grow and grow until it became an overwhelming problem.

Alan: What steps did the vendor take to address the problem?

Rachel: He promised us that these were just temporary glitches, but they didn't go away, and pretty soon we came to believe that this was the cost of speed.

Alan: That's pretty concerning to me, because it seems to me that what you need in a situation like this is both speed and accuracy. Is that right?

Rachel: Right. It's great that you say you can hold the time between when the order's received and when it ships to 45 minutes, but that doesn't do us any good if half the orders are sent out with the wrong materials.

Alan: So you're looking for speed, accuracy, and a way of checking to make sure both of these elements are there. Is that right?

Rachel: Yes. That's it.

Alan: Well, let me tell you in a little more detail about the process by which we fulfill orders. When the order is received, it automatically goes to that section of the warehouse where the product is housed.

Rachel: How does that happen?

Alan: That's based on the code words that you include with the order. The order shows up on a screen at the central booking station for that section of the warehouse, and a runner picks the appropriate product and prints out a packing slip for it. That slip is viewed by a checker—

Rachel: You mean someone actually stands there and checks the packing slip against the order?

Alan: That's right. The packing slip, which is based on the original order, includes the code words. Each product also includes a label with the appropriate code word, and all of these products are scanned by the checker so that if there's an error it will be detected immediately. Only then is the order packaged and placed on a belt to transfer it to shipping.

Rachel: That sounds like a good system, but are there still errors?

Alan: We average one error per 30,000 orders shipped. And if the wrong package goes out, we will do overnight shipping to the customer of the correct item without additional charge.

Rachel: That sounds good. I'm glad you're concerned about QC.

Alan: Well, we are. As you say, it doesn't help you if an unacceptable percentage of your orders shipped are wrong. That reflects badly on us as well as you. We also have a decentralized system that works very well to speed up delivery times. We do this by integrating clients into our warehouse structure. Your products will be housed at depots in the Midwest, Southwest, West Coast, and Northeast.

Okay, that's more like it! Alan has correctly perceived that Rachel's main concern is quality control. So he's done a very sensible thing: He's started asking questions about why she's not happy with her existing vendor. Remember that if you're selling to a new client, you're in a conversation because she's not happy with how things are being handled by her current supplier. So the first thing you have to do is find out why. Once Alan has determined what the problem is with QC and has addressed Rachel's concerns, he can get the discussion back to what he perceives is a strong point of his pitch: the decentralized warehousing system that improves order placed to order delivered times. At this point Rachel's prepared to listen to him talk about this because he's listened to her main issue and offered an answer to it.

So remember: Communicating starts with active listening.

THE IMPORTANCE
OF GOOD LISTENING 15

A couple of weeks ago, I was making my way out of the apartment on my way to work. It was a Friday morning, as I recall, and I had a lot of end-of-the-week stuff on my mind. My wife was in the kitchen, putting the breakfast dishes in the dishwasher, when she called out something to me.

Now, as I say, my mind was elsewhere. I was in a hurry. I had two important meetings, both of them some distance away. And it was raining.

All of which is to say that I wasn't paying much attention. What I heard was, "See you this evening, Steve."

What my wife actually said to me, according to her later recollection, was, "Steve, don't forget we're going out to dinner with Bob and Janice this evening. You won't have time to come home, since our reservations are at six o'clock. You're going to go straight to the restaurant after you drop off the car. And remember that the restaurant just moved—it's on 23rd Street now, not 21st Street. I've got a meeting that lasts until 5:30, so you won't be able to reach me by phone. I'll see you there, Steve."

I'm one of those people who needs to put things down in his calendar. Appointments and phone calls don't have a reality for me until they appear written down at the proper time and date. Naturally, I'd forgotten all about Bob and Janice, dinner, the restaurant, and my wife's meeting. I hadn't written it down; ipso facto, it didn't exist.

I finished the day's meetings and sales calls and dragged myself wearily back to the apartment, looking forward to a restful evening spent in slippers in front of the television—maybe with dinner on a tray. What I found was no wife, no dinner, no tray—just an empty apartment and a nagging feeling at the back of my mind that I was supposed to be somewhere else.

I'll draw a discreet veil over the rest of the evening, since it was nearly seven when I remembered about dinner. Fortunately, my wife is of a forgiving disposition—she has to be, to be married to me. However, I'm sure I'm going to hear about that evening for some time to come.

ENGAGE IN ACTIVE LISTENING

What happened to me was an extreme case of not listening. I suspect that there have been very few, if any, times when such a thing happened to you during a sales call. Nonetheless, a lot of sales are lost or weakened by the inability of the salesperson to engage in what I would call "active listening."

This sounds like a contradiction in terms, doesn't it? After all, isn't listening an inherently passive activity? Isn't the whole point of listening to not talk and to sit quietly while the other person talks?

Well, not quite. What I'm going to suggest is that active listening accomplishes three important goals:

1. It demonstrates to the person doing the talking that you're actually listening, not nodding your head in agreement while all the while thinking about your lunch plans.

2. It exposed and clarifies any points of disagreement between you so that you can resolve them.

3. It allows conversational openings for moving the discussion forward.

The principles of active listening are pretty simple:

1. When someone is talking to you, listen with your whole body. That means turning toward the person, looking him or her in the face (but not staring with an unblinking gaze; that's just creepy), and occasionally nodding. Your body should be relaxed but attentive. You can lean forward a bit from time to time, but don't do it suddenly or compulsively. Avoid fiddling with a pencil, paper clip, or some other bit of trivia. Fiddling shows boredom.

2. Give verbal cues that you're paying attention. "Uh huh," and "I see" are perfectly fine. You don't have to do this after every sentence; in fact, it's better that you do not do so, since that'll get annoying quickly. But make sure the person to whom you're listening knows you're thinking about what he or she is saying.

3. Take notes. Either jot down some relevant information on a pad or type into your smartphone or computer (I'm old-fashioned enough to prefer a pen and paper approach, because I think it's less intrusive and impersonal). Often what you write isn't nearly as important as the fact that you think what the client is saying is important enough to take a note about.

4. Mirror the client's statements. When he or she comes to a logical stopping point, say something along the lines of, "I see. So what you're saying is . . ." and give it back to

the speaker. Don't use identical words to those the client used, or you can come across as mocking and insincere. This stage is extremely important, because this is where you can use what the client has said to draw some further conclusions and take the discussion onto a new level.

5. As the conversation progresses, refer back to what the client has said previously. If you don't do that, the impression you give is of someone with a canned presentation who doesn't give a damn what the client thinks. Too often I've seen salespeople who were so pleased with the presentation they'd crafted in the seclusion of their offices that they might as well have been speaking to a mannequin for all the attention they paid their audience members. Phrases such as "As you said earlier" get you away from this sort of thing.

All these techniques begin from the standpoint that you should encourage the client to do most of the talking. Elsewhere I've alluded to the 80-20 rule in sales calls—the standard you should aim for is that the client should do about 80 percent of the talking, and you should do 20 percent. This is especially important for sales calls when you're first making a client's acquaintance. In such a situation, your main goal is to learn about the client:

- What is her background?
- How does she view her customer base?
- How does she view her industry?
- What are her plans for growing her business?
- What problems is she currently experiencing?

If you can get the answers to these five questions, you're well on the way to making a sale.

BENEFITS OF ACTIVE LISTENING

Let's come back to the three reasons I mentioned earlier for developing active listening skills.

1. **Active listening demonstrates to the person doing the talking that you're actually listening, not nodding your head in agreement while all the while thinking about your lunch plans.** This is important both because you do really want to listen to what the client is saying—you'll find yourself on your way out the door very quickly if you don't—and because you want to give him or her confidence in you. Sales calls aren't merely about making the sale that day; they're about building a long-term relationship with the client. If you don't really care enough to do that, you'll probably make a lot of sales over the course of a year or so, but when you come back to these people the following year you won't get anywhere. Any good salesperson wants to build a strong, vital client base. Active listening helps show the client that you're someone who's genuinely interested in what he or she has to say.

    It's possible, of course, that some clients (for instance, those addicted to a passive style of communication—see Chapter 13) will drive you around the bend with their long, winding way of discussing any subject. In such situations, you've got to avoid showing obvious signs of impatience and use your active listening skills to move them carefully closer to the point.

2. **Active listening exposes and clarifies any points of disagreement between you so that you can resolve them.** I've said elsewhere that the place where all latent disagreements and issues are inevitably forced to the

surface is the contract stage of the sale. That's because when the pencil hits the paper, there's no way to avoid disagreements. So wouldn't it be best if you could avoid conflict at this stage and instead resolve disagreements early on in the sale?

If you're really listening to what the client is saying, you can note right away any place in the discussion that's likely to cause trouble later on. You can tell also if the client is trying to paper over an issue or paint something in rosier colors than it deserves. In general, my thinking is that it's always better to deal with issues earlier in a sale than later. That way, there will be fewer (or no) surprises at the contract stage when both sides have already committed significant resources to the deal.

If you find yourself concerned over a point the client brings up, there's no need to fly off the handle or interrupt. Instead, wait until the client has finished talking and then say something along the lines of, "I noticed when you referred to the question of delivery discounts, you indicated .... I'm not sure that's something we can agree to without ....". If you've listened carefully to the client you'll also be in a position at this point to propose a positive alternative rather than letting the disagreement hang in the air.

3. **Active listening allows conversational openings for moving the discussion forward.** Most of the time, the client is going to look to you to figure out where the sales conversation should go (although an exception to this can be made in the case of aggressive communicators). The more carefully you listen, the easier it will be to figure out the next logical step.

To do this, find out the problems the client is facing. Then, ask her to prioritize them—not in terms of time to solve them but in terms of their importance. It's best if, based on your listening, you can yourself indicate what you think are the biggest problems and how important they are.

Assuming the client agrees with you about this, you're now in a position to explain exactly how the service offered by your company will help solve the client's most important problem. Thus you've gotten the conversation started on the next track, the one in which you propose specific terms for the sale.

ACTIVE LISTENING IS AN ART

Active listening is an acquired art. The more you do it, the better you get. Furthermore, it's highly interactive. People have told me from time to time that what makes someone interesting is that he or she says interesting things. I tend to disagree with this. The people I find the most interesting and engaging are those who show the most interest in what other people have to say and who interact with others in a friendly and fascinating fashion. Those are the kinds of people who invariably make the sales and win the commissions.

CLIENT CHALLENGE: "DO YOU UNDERSTAND WHAT I NEED?"

16

Sales, I find the longer I'm in it, can be largely about egos. I admit that I have what I regard as a healthy ego. Some people might say it's inflated, but I think on balance that I understand and appreciate my strengths and weaknesses. I'm not given to boasting (at least, I don't think so), but I also know that I'm very, very good at what I do. I resent anyone who challenges that, and I'm always ready to defend my long experience of sales training.

At the same time, I understand that there are moments in sales when you have to take whatever ego you've got and put it in your back pocket for a few minutes. Even if you know what's best for the client, even if you're absolutely sure that what he's saying is complete baloney, you can't come right out and tell him that. If you do, you can be sure that his ego will bump up against yours and in no time at all you'll be pushing and shoving at one another.

The whole thing reminds me of the Japanese sport of sumo wrestling. Two gigantic men, each clad in a skimpy loincloth, rush together and attempt to push each other out of the ring. I've been to see a match once while on a business trip to Japan and came away with a certain appreciation for the finer points of the sport coupled with a conviction that nothing was ever going to drag me to another match.

WHEN EGOS MEET

Sales calls that go wrong can seem like a sumo match. At a certain point, salesperson and client start pushing against one another, each determined to be the winner, each steady as a rock in his conviction that there's only one person in the room who's right, and it's him. Unless something or someone intervenes, chances are that such sales calls are going to end badly with the salesperson slamming the door on his way out while the client deletes the salesperson's phone number from his list of telephone contacts.

Here's a conversation between George and Rich. George is a salesperson selling an accounting service, while Rich runs a chain of electronics stores. I've heard a lot of exchanges like this, and believe me, they never end well.

> **George:** Frankly, it's a bit surprising to me that you guys have stayed afloat as long as you have, considering the subpar accounting that you seem to be getting.

> **Rich:** Actually, I think we've done pretty well. In fact, we've done more than well . . . we're considered a significant player in our field.

> **George:** But look at the crap you're letting happen to your books. You've been audited in four of the last six years. Maybe you're satisfied with that kind of thing, but my company isn't. We know we can do a better job for you than the "accountants" you've got working for you now.

Rich: I don't think those audits were a big deal at all. We came out squeaky clean in two of them, and with the other two the auditors found very minor mistakes.

George: Those "minor" mistakes cost you guys more than $15,000 in back taxes. That doesn't sound minor to me.

Rich: Look, you've got no idea what it's like on the front lines—

George: Oh, don't hit me with that crap! I've seen companies that were 10 times bigger than yours who were glad to get our accounting package. In fact, I've sold to ABC Corporation, and their revenues were $250 million last year.

Rich: You know, that kind of thing doesn't impress me at all. I happen to know that ABC Corporation is having some significant financial problems, and I wonder how much your accounting had to do with that.

George: Look, here's the thing. You can sit and listen to what I've got to say, or we can just end this right now.

Rich: It's ended. Don't let the door hit you on the way out!

Well . . . I told you it wasn't going to end well. The whole thing reminds me of a comedy routine I once saw in which a bunch of well-off guys are talking about how hard they had it as kids.

"Hah!" says one. "When I was a kid we had to walk 10 miles every morning to school."

"You got to go to school?" says another. "We would have loved to go to school. We had to walk 20 miles to our jobs in a factory!"

"You mean you had jobs?" chimes in a third. "My God, we would have killed to have jobs. When I was a kid, our parents used to beat us when we got up and send us out on a 30-mile hike to bring back other kids to be beaten."

And so on.

It's an exaggeration, of course, but reread the sales call dialogue. Doesn't it call this sort of thing to mind? At some point it stops being a sales call and becomes a ridiculous exercise in ego puffing. Neither Rich nor George is interested, in the end, in solving a problem or selling a service. Instead, they're too busy demonstrating who's got the most power and authority.

This being a sales call in which George is trying to convince Rich to do something—namely, to buy the service he's selling—it's inevitable that George will come out on the losing side. But Rich loses as well, because now he won't have access to what could be a superior accounting system to the one he's using. In the end, everyone loses.

HOW EGO CAN SABOTAGE A SALES CALL

What are the main things that went wrong?

1. George starts out by attacking the client—never a good move. George may think Rich's business is hanging by a thread, but it's a very bad idea to say so. It has the predictable result of putting Rich on the defensive. Now he thinks he's got to justify all his decisions, good, bad, and indifferent. George and Rich are now antagonists rather than partners.

2. George name drops, tossing out the fact that he's provided services for ABC Corporation. This is wrong on two counts: First, telling someone about a much bigger company that you've done business with implies that his problems aren't that important, something no client wants to hear. Second, it's a golden rule of salesmanship to never, never, never discuss the business affairs of another client. George doesn't quite give away crucial information about the ABC Corporation, but he's starting to ride that dangerous train.

3. Once the call starts to go wrong, George makes no effort to correct the problem. This is what I meant earlier about the role of ego in bad sales. It's obvious that Rich is angry and striking back at what he sees as George's attacks. Instead of retreating and refocusing the conversation, George pushes his ego even further. Rich, of course, has a strong ego to begin with; you don't get to be an executive without an ability to be assertive. For both men at this point the call has become an exercise in who's got the biggest ego. Who's the strongest guy in the sumo ring? My response is, who cares? Just get the damn sale!

Elsewhere I've discussed the role of anger in sales negotiation. Getting angry can be a useful tactic sometimes if you use it to make a point or to assert a dominant role in a negotiation. But at the stage George and Rich are at, the only thing anger does is escalate. The sale has nowhere to go, and Rich quickly brings it to an end.

BYPASS EGO TO PURSUE YOUR GOAL

Let's start with the basics: What does George want to do?

1. He wants to convey that his company can provide a significant improvement in accounting performance over what Rich has been receiving.

2. He wants to convince Rich that he's got the chops to deliver on his promise of superior performance.

3. He wants to move the sale to the next stage.

With these things in mind, consider how the discussion could have gone.

George: In reviewing your company's history, I see that you've been audited by the IRS for four of the past six years. I wonder if you could tell me something about how that happened.

Rich: Well, two of the audits didn't turn up anything, and we passed with flying colors. Two of them found some problems.

George: Did you have to pay back taxes?

Rich: Yes, $20,000 in total. To be frank, that's the reason we started to look around for someone who might be able to do a better job.

George: Yes, I can see why you'd want to do that. I think we can offer a level of service that you'll find to be an improvement over your current accounting firm.

Rich: How much experience have you had with this sort of thing?

George: Quite a lot. We've provided services for a number of companies with revenues similar to yours. In all these cases, we've been able to find ways of saving them money on their tax bills as well as giving them timely information on the state of their finances. What's especially important to me is to find out exactly what you want from our service so I can see how we can best provide it.

Rich: Sure. I think we can do business together.

Now we're getting somewhere. I assume that George, who's a conscientious salesperson, has done his research in advance. He knows—it's a matter of public record—that Rich's company has been audited four times. But he wants to get Rich to open up about the nature of the problems.

Once Rich has identified the main problem he's trying to solve—that is, that the tax advice he's been given is bad—George is in a position to achieve his first goal. He can assure Rich that his company won't make the sorts of errors that resulted in a $20,000 tax bill.

Rich, of course, wants some support for this statement. So George gives it to him, but without being specific. If Rich pushes on this, George may have to give out some names. He may even have a list of testimonials from companies who've used his service. But he doesn't name drop, and he doesn't appear on the brink of disclosing confidential information about anyone. This marks him as trustworthy and reassures Rich that he's dealing with a professional.

Finally, George does something throughout the interview that he didn't do in our first version: he asks questions. Even if he knows the answer, he asks questions. The idea is to get the client talking and to get the client to identify the problem and its probable solution. This is what I mean by taking the sale to the next level. The two men have moved away from the introductory phase of the sale, where they've figured out the problem, and are now ready to discuss solutions.

Dealing with a client with a big ego is often difficult. But most of the time the best thing you can do is not to respond to provocations. Putting your ego up against his will make you feel good for a little while, but it won't win you the sale. And isn't that the whole point of selling?

SELLING A PERSONAL RELATIONSHIP

17

Back in the dim and distant past of the early 1970s, when the world was still divided into the two hostile camps of East and West, the leader of the Free World was a man who had cut his political teeth as an ardent anticommunist. During the 1950s, he'd been a leader of the forces within the U.S. Senate sniffing out communism at home and abroad. His first campaign for senator was against the California incumbent, Helen Gahagan Douglas, whom he described, in a telling phrase, as "pink right down to her underwear." Douglas lost and passed into a historical footnote. The victor in the race went on to become vice president in the Eisenhower administration, where he continued his anticommunist activities. After several attempts, at last in 1968 he was elected president of the United States.

His name, of course, was Richard Nixon.

Now with that background, imagine the amazement when in 1972 Nixon announced that he would be the first American president to travel to China. The impact was stunning—and it was not just that an American leader was traveling to China, which had, since the 1949 revolution, been a largely closed society about which most Americans knew little. No, the real impact was that the leader going there was Nixon. His visit, which included conversations with Chairman Mao, state banquets, and a stroll along the Great Wall, began to break down the barriers to communication between America and China. (Today, we're still to an extent adjusting to that relationship with the vast expansion of our trade with China.) Nixon even seemed to establish a friendship of sorts with the Chinese leader Zhou Enlai.

Nixon also traveled a number of times to the Soviet Union (this, of course, was back when there was a Soviet Union to travel to). He forged a strong relationship with its leader, Leonid Brezhnev, head of the Communist Party. If you think this is a weird turn of events, then you're no more surprised than most of us were back in the 1970s, watching these events unfold.

Nixon's own response to this incongruity was that it was these personal relationships that he had established with men of power on the other side of the Iron Curtain that enabled him to be effective as president. He, Brezhnev, Mao, and Zhou belonged to an exclusive club, one that routinely discussed and resolved matters affecting billions of people around the globe. This was either reassuring or very scary, depending on your point of view. In any event, it's interesting to wonder what might have happened if the Watergate scandal hadn't led to Nixon's resignation in 1974.

I bring this up because in this chapter we're going to talk about the importance of a personal relationship between you and your client. I'm not suggesting that this relationship is on the order of two heads of state—I mean, let's keep things in perspective. But in one sense all personal relationships in business are the same: They should enhance your business relationship, not compete with it. Above all, they should never set up a situation in which the two come into conflict.

At the same time, particularly when it comes to services, selling a personal relationship to the client is an exceedingly valuable thing to do. Because clients want to know that you're willing to step outside the bounds of a normal business relationship and go that extra mile to make sure they're happy and that their best interests are being served. A personal relationship is also valuable because the better you know your clients, the better able you'll be to figure out their business problems and help to solve them, which is the reason you're in the sales business.

TWO EXAMPLES OF PERSONAL RELATIONSHIPS WITH CLIENTS

I can illustrate the advantages and disadvantages of forging personal relationships with your clients through two examples from my own experience—one positive and one negative.

Several years ago, I was negotiating with a difficult client. I'm used to tough negotiations, but this one was a standout even for me. Every time I came up with a proposal, the client countered with something else. When I said A, he said A-plus. When I said yes, he said no way. I felt, after several sessions, that we were starting to go around in circles. Nevertheless, I pushed hard because this was an important deal to me and because I had a sense—just some sort of intuition—that there was a deal to be reached if we could get to it.

During the wind-down of one of our sessions, we were both irritated and exhausted. I said something that revealed my state of mind, and he sighed deeply.

"Sorry, Steve," he said. "My daughter's getting married next month, and I've got a million things on my mind."

Now, it so happened that my daughter had been married the previous year. I asked where his daughter's wedding was taking place. The church, as it turned out, was one that my daughter had looked at as a possible venue for her wedding. We started chatting about weddings and how nerve-racking they can be, particularly for the father of the bride. That led us to a discussion of children and their discontents. At some point, he glanced at his watch and said, "Listen, do you want to get a bite to eat?"

I said sure, and we found a local restaurant. There, over a meal and several drinks, we began forging what was to become a long friendship. We found out many things we had in common. We found points of difference. (I believe firmly that if you don't disagree with your friends about at least a few things, the friendship is unlikely to last.) Above all, we spent several hours talking about everything except work.

The next day, when we picked up our negotiations, things went more smoothly. There were still issues to hammer out, but the testiness and latent hostility that had underlaid our previous discussions was gone. We finished the deal and, over the course of the next several years, our friendship continued to grow. My wife and I still see him and his spouse; we've gone to plays and concerts and movies together, and we've wandered the streets of Manhattan after sitting up late in a bar drinking and laughing together.

When it comes to business, he and I know how to separate our personal connections from our professional ones. However, we don't pretend that those personal connections don't exist or aren't important. The main thing that's happened, and that started to happen in that first meal we ate together, is that we trust each other. I know that when he takes a stand in a negotiation, it's because he genuinely thinks it's the best position for his company. And he knows that when I try to get a concession from him, I'm not being dishonest or trying to make things more difficult. The essence of our personal relationship is trust, which makes sales easier.

Now to the negative example.

A while back a friend of mine started a business. It grew swiftly because she knew what she was doing and she hired very smart people. In what seemed like no time at all, she was the head of a thriving concern with a growing sales force. That's when she came to me and asked if I would put together some training sessions for her salespeople.

I told her I'd be glad to do so and that I was pretty sure I could help her salespeople move to the next level of sales. In short, everything was sweetness and light. She readily agreed to my fee, and I set up the session.

About six months or so after the training had taken place, I got a phone call from her.

"I'm very upset with you," she began.

"Why's that?"

"You guaranteed an 8 to 10 percent jump in revenue numbers as a result of your training. I've been going over the quarterly numbers, and I'm not seeing anything like that."

"Now wait a minute," I told her. "I never guaranteed that level of increase. What I said was that this sort of training can often result in an increase in revenue of between 8 and 10 percent. But that isn't an ironclad guarantee, and besides, it often takes time."

"Dammit, Steve!" she snapped. "I accepted your word on this, and now you've let me down. I know this wasn't in the contract, but we're friends, and I assumed you'd give me the straight truth. Now look where it's got me! I've got backers coming next week to look at my books, and they're going to want to see much better numbers before they decide to invest more capital."

"I'm sorry," I replied. "But I have to stand on my answer. If you look at the terms of your contract—"

There was a sharp "click" as she hung up the phone.

Fifteen minutes later, my wife called me. "What did you do to your friend?" she asked. "I just got a call from her canceling our dinner next weekend, and when I asked her why, she said, 'Ask Steve!'"

I tried calling my friend (now rapidly becoming my former friend) back, but she wouldn't take my phone calls. Shortly after, I heard that she'd signed up for more sales training with one of my rivals. I never heard from her again.

SOME GUIDELINES FOR CLIENT RELATIONSHIPS

As you can see, it's all too easy to blur the lines between a friend-ship or a personal relationship of any kind and a business relation-ship. Nonetheless, I think where it's appropriate it's well worth pursuing a broader, deeper relationship with a client for all the reasons I mentioned earlier.

There are, of course, circumstances in which you should not do this.

1. If a personal relationship with the client could be reason-ably interpreted by a third party as a conflict of interest for either of you. Under these circumstances, you're likely to wind up in a very bad place if you don't know how to distinguish between what's appropriate and what's not.

2. Any sort of romantic relationship with a client is right off the table. If you're good friends with a client and that friendship develops into something more, that's great and I'm very happy for you, but you can't sell to him anymore.

3. If a personal relationship with the client is perceived by oth-ers within your organization or that of the client as wrong or inappropriate, it's probably a good thing to step back.

With this in mind, here are some suggestions:

1. When talking to clients, try to find out something about them as people. You don't want to be rude or intrusive, but most people will appreciate your interest in their lives and open up to you.

2. Try to schedule at least one or two meetings with a client in a less formal setting than a conference room. Restaurants can be your friends in this regard, but if you want to eat a

meal together, find a restaurant where you can make your-
selves heard without shouting above the waiters, kitchen
staff, or band.

3. Don't be shy about mentioning your own extra-business
   interests. You'll be surprised at how many new friends you
   can make that way.

Do this, and in no time at all you may find yourself walking along the Great Wall of China and saying to your guide, "It is
indeed a great wall!"

CLIENT CHALLENGE: "HOW DO I KNOW YOU'LL BE THERE FOR US?"

18

Remember Marlene Dietrich?

Probably not; most people don't these days. This is one reason I don't go to the movies very much anymore. I've become disillusioned with Hollywood—not that I had that many illusions to begin with. But these days it seems, more and more, that nothing gets to the big screen unless it's got lots of explosions, foul language, nudity (or something close to it), and killer robots.

Back in the great days of movies, movies were about something. Movie stars dominated the screen by the sheer force of their personalities, by the charisma they brought to the picture.

To me, Dietrich was the embodiment of this. She started her career on stage in Germany in the 1920s, and then came to America to make it big in movies. She was prevented from returning to Germany by the rise of Nazism and the outbreak of World War II, so she stayed on in the United States and became even bigger as a cabaret artist, working out of Vegas and other flashy locations.

I bring up Dietrich partly because I like her and enjoy an

excuse to talk about her, but also because of something she once said: "It's the friends you can call up at 4 a.m. that matter."

Which brings me to the subject of this chapter, something that's extremely important in selling services: What kind of relationship are you going to have with the client after you've concluded the deal? Are you going to be a voice on the phone, someone who vanishes after completing negotiations and is never heard from again? Or are you going to be a 4 a.m. friend—someone the client can turn to if he has a problem with what your company is doing and knows that no matter what he asks you he'll get a straight, honest answer.

Obviously I advise being the second kind of salesperson—not merely because I think being a 4 a.m. friend is a good moral choice, but because it makes better sense from the standpoint of getting the sale. Later, when I discuss customer service and its importance (Chapter 29), I'll explain how tales of bad customer service can spread like a virus, poisoning everything they touch. For now I want to look at two instances of a client-salesperson relationship: one in which the salesperson puts the client first and one in which he doesn't.

THE TAX MAN COMETH

Let's look in on a tax preparation company. It's April 14, the day before taxes are due, and Jenny is preparing to leave the office for the day when her phone rings.

Jenny: Hello?

Roger: Hi, Jenny. Thank goodness I got hold of you. This is Roger Partridge from Partridge Appliances.

Jenny: Uh . . . just remind me.

Roger: You sold us your tax preparation package late last year. We're out in Smithville . . . it was in October of last year . . .

Jenny: Oh, uh, sure. Yes, I believe I do remember you. What's going on, Roger?

Roger: I've got a big problem. We sent our preparation packet in to your accountant two months ago and didn't hear back or anything. When I called a week ago, I was told you were still working on the taxes. I still haven't heard anything, and now taxes are due tomorrow. I don't know what to do.

Jenny: Did you contact your preparation accountant? That'd be . . . uh . . .

Roger: David Ashley. Yes, I sent him a couple of e-mails and left phone messages, but he hasn't returned my last couple of calls. I'm really in a panic here, Jenny. I don't know what to do. We have to get these forms in tomorrow, or we're really in trouble.

Jenny: Well, to be honest, Roger, I don't know what I can do to help you. I'm really just on the sales side of things, and I don't have any way of knowing exactly what your tax situation is.

Roger: Well, I don't know either, but all I know is that when you made the sale to us of this package you said it would take care of our corporate taxes without any worries. I'm worried now, Jenny. And I'd like to know what you and your company are going to do to fix the problem.

Jenny: Look, I'll leave a message for my boss. I'm sure someone will get back to you tomorrow and make sure it's all worked out. But I'm on my way out of the office right now.

Roger: Now wait just a damn minute—

Jenny: That's really all I can do.

I don't know about you, but I have a feeling that Roger's company is going to be facing a hefty penalty from the IRS for nonfiling of tax returns. In all likelihood, depending on the precise wording of the contract he signed with Jenny's company, he'll be taking the tax preparers to court for negligent business practices. And so he should. What Jenny's doing here is unconscionable.

To begin at the beginning, it's quite obvious at the start of the phone call that Jenny has no idea who Roger is or of anything about the sale. Now, we don't all have fantastic memories—I'm the first to admit that mine isn't improving with age—but there's still no excuse for the kind of fumbling and mumbling that Jenny displays at the beginning of this conversation. The minute Roger gives his name and the name of his company, she should be sitting at her computer, pulling up his file and scanning it to get a good idea of the most important things about his company. There's nothing wrong with saying something like, "Just give me a minute here, Roger, to pull up your file so I have all the facts and figures in front of me." In fact, that's important because it shows you care about what the client is telling you and want to make sure you give him accurate information.

Second, Jenny's obvious immediate instinct, rather than trying to get a few more details out of Roger about his problem, is to try to foist the issue off on someone else. Let me be very clear here. There's nothing wrong with you referring a client to someone else in your organization if that someone else is better positioned to help him or her. In fact, usually that's the responsible thing to do, since there's little or no point in attempting to fix a problem you don't understand.

The difficulty here is that Jenny hasn't bothered to ask Roger any questions, so she doesn't really know much about the problem beyond his immediate description of it. She makes it obvious to him that she doesn't care very much.

Third, Jenny never expresses any sympathy with Roger's

concern—in fact, at this point it's a bit more than concern, it's full-blown panic.

People used to (and still do) make fun of Bill Clinton. I myself had and have a lot of questions and disagreements with his political decisions. But one thing he was very good at when he was president was sympathizing with other people's predicaments. The most famous example is his statement, "I feel your pain." And somehow his listeners believed he did.

Jenny doesn't have to go quite that far, but she does need Roger to understand that she knows why he's upset and that she's concerned as well.

Then Jenny says something no salesperson should ever say: "I don't know what I can do to help you."

Strike those words from your vocabulary. There's always something you can do to help. It may not solve the problem, but it will get the client closer to a solution. The minute you say you can't help anymore, you might as well hang up the phone and never plan to hear from the client again. After all, why should he call you? When it was 4 a.m. and he needed you, you weren't there.

HOW TO BE A 4 A.M. FRIEND TO YOUR CLIENT

Now let's listen in again, this time assuming that Jenny has absorbed the lessons of this chapter and has a better grasp of what she's doing.

Jenny: Hello?

Roger: Hi, Jenny. Thank goodness I got hold of you. This is Roger Partridge from Partridge Appliances.

Jenny: Oh, yes, Roger. Good to speak with you again. I remember you, but not all the details of the sale. Can you give me a minute to pull up your file?

Roger: Sure.

Jenny: Okay, here it is. I see you're out in Smithville, and you purchased our basic corporate tax preparation package last October. How's that working for you?

Roger: Not good. I've got a big problem. We sent our preparation packet in to your accountant two months ago and didn't hear back or anything. When I called a week ago, I was told you were still working on the taxes. I still haven't heard anything, and now taxes are due tomorrow. I don't know what to do.

Jenny: Oh, dear. That's a big problem. I can certainly understand why you're upset. I see from the file that your accountant contact here is David Ashley. Has he not been in touch with you?

Roger: No. And he hasn't returned my calls. That's why I called you.

Jenny: Well, I'm sorry David hasn't been in touch with you, but I'm glad you got me. I'm sure we can figure out what the next step is. Has anyone discussed filing an extension with you?

Roger: No.

Jenny: Okay. The paperwork's pretty straightforward, but it's not my area of expertise. Lou Martin, another of our accountants, does this kind of thing all the time for clients. Let me see if he's still in the office, okay?

Roger: Okay.

[Short break]

Jenny: Okay, I just spoke to Lou. He'll file an extension on your behalf so we can get this whole thing straightened out without the pressure of time. He's going to take some information from you and then walk you through the procedure. Is that okay?

Roger: Yes, that would be fine.

Jenny: Okay. Before I switch you to him, I just want to apologize for this snafu. I can assure you it's not typical, and we'll look into what happened so it doesn't occur again. I'll speak to David and find out what the problem was.

Roger: I appreciate that.

Jenny: If I may, I'd like to give you a call back tomorrow and make sure things are going okay. Would 10 a.m. be all right?

Roger: That would be great. Thank you.

Whew! Crisis averted. Roger's no longer angry with Jenny because he's been given a plan of action that includes a follow-up. Jenny hasn't tried to solve the problem herself, something that could have been disastrous unless she's an expert in tax law; rather, she's found someone who can take care of the problem. Notice as well that she hasn't blamed anyone for the issue—not even the person who was supposed to call Roger back and didn't. The blame game is easy to play in sales sometimes, because it always seems easier to make it the other guy's fault. But in the end, that sort of thing will come back to bite you.

Always remember: The sale doesn't end with the closing. It doesn't end with signing the contract. A sale is an ongoing, living thing. And when there's a problem, you may well be the client's first point of contact with your company.

When that happens, you'd better be a 4 a.m. friend. And now, if you'll excuse me, *Witness for the Prosecution* is on television. Ah, Dietrich!

BUILDING
CONFIDENCE

19

S elling, as I've never ceased to say for the past thirty-some years, doesn't just depend on one thing. It's a combination of lots of different skills and attitudes that when put together form something greater than the sum of its parts. Binding all these elements together is something intangible, something that good salespeople learn through long experience and hone into a winning style.

It's possible that in your organization you'll see that some salespeople always seem to get the great commissions and sign the big deals. They're the ones who get praised in the company newsletter, who work their way up the corporate ladder, and who, on occasion, get the corner office. It's customary to say that people like that are "born salespeople."

To which, I reply, "Hogwash!"

I've never seen anyone who came into this world with an inherent ability to sell. There's no "sales gene" that scientists have discovered, no magical ability to close the deal, no weird cologne or perfume you can put on in the morning that will make clients swoon and scribble their names on contracts. If such a thing existed, believe me, someone would have packaged it, put a label on it, and would be selling it to people like you and me.

I believe that selling is an acquired skill and that given the proper training, *anyone can be a successful salesperson.* It takes dedication and commitment, as well as a very smart teacher or mentor.

And it takes confidence—which is what this chapter is about.

WHY YOU NEED CONFIDENCE

Why talk about confidence in a book about selling services? Because in selling a service, you're selling a promise of a future benefit. Most services, such as accounting, bookkeeping, sales, fulfillment, and so forth will bring a benefit to the client in the future, and that future can seem as if it's a very long way away sometimes. But you, the salesperson, have to be able to instill in clients the confidence that purchasing your service will benefit them, even if it takes weeks, months, or years to realize those benefits. And in order to give clients that confidence, you've got to have it yourself.

Back in 1952, Norman Vincent Peale published *The Power of Positive Thinking.* In some ways it was one of the first modern self-help books, and when you go into a bookstore and stare at the hundreds of titles you find on the self-help shelves—everything from books on dieting for happiness to suggestions that you can improve your finances through yoga—you're looking at Peale's legacy. His book sold around 5 million copies over the years with its breezy message, a combination of religion and pop psychology. (The book was attacked by many professional psychologists when it was published, but that didn't stop it from becoming popular; in fact, it probably helped.) Peale's basic message was that positive thinking can make a difference in your life. If you start off with confidence (and a belief in God), things will get better for you.

Without going much of the way with Norman Vincent Peale, I can say that the essence of this message isn't a bad starting place for salespeople. Confidence is, indeed, key to successful selling, and that confidence starts inside you. You have to believe in yourself, believe in your company, and believe in what you're selling.

Let's start with confidence in yourself. I know some people who get out of bed in the morning already feeling defeated. They're convinced that nothing is going to go right for them, that their day is going to be one long series of disasters, ending in a complete train wreck. You know how a conversation with one of these people is going to go when you encounter them at the watercooler in the office.

"Hey, George. How's it going?"

"Okay, I guess."

"Got anything interesting on this morning?"

"No. Same old routine."

"Any interesting prospects on the horizon?"

"Nope. No one's interested in what I'm selling." [pause] "God, I hate this place!"

It's hardly surprising that anyone with that attitude is going to have a difficult day. I have a theory that we carry around our own little atmospheric bubble. Some people walk into a room and the sun comes out, birds start singing, and in the distance you can hear a band playing. Other people will walk into the same room and a little black cloud will appear over everyone's head. Guess who's more likely to get a sale?

HOW TO INCREASE YOUR CONFIDENCE

If you start every day with a conviction that you can overcome obstacles and can accomplish what's on your to-do list, you'll find that you're happier and that better things happen to you. No one likes being around a perpetual gloom machine. On the other hand, people are naturally drawn to confidence and optimism. Strive to be someone who emanates the latter qualities.

Regarding your company, some people may think I'm advocating that you act as a corporate shill for whatever foolish decisions the front office may have made, but that's not it at all. You don't have to be a bubble-headed cheerleader for your company. Nor do you have to be an apologist. If your company (or you) has made a mistake, you need to apologize, fix the problem, and move on. But if you believe that what your company does is genuinely worth doing, you'll see that it's much easier to convince other people of this as well.

For that reason, I suggest that you sit down and make a list of the things your company does. What services does it provide? Then, after each service, list how many people are directly affected by that service. That is, how many people does your company touch directly on a daily basis?

Now here's a trickier bit: put down the number of people who are indirectly affected by the services your company provides. You can be pretty expansive here. For instance, if you work for a landscaping company that services corporate office buildings, the people who are directly affected are the people who work in those buildings. Those indirectly affected will include those who merely visit those buildings, those who see the buildings, even if it's just passing by on a bus. As well, people indirectly affected might include the workers who create the materials your company uses—in the case of a landscaping company, the mulch, sod, topsoil, gardening tools, and so on.

You'll find that you're starting to come up with some very big numbers. But you have to think about what this means. These are the people my company touches daily, directly or indirectly. What would happen if we went away tomorrow? How much of a difference would it make? Would people miss us? Would they talk about it?

The greatest thing a company can strive for, I believe, is to make a difference. The late Steve Jobs ran Apple in a way that made a huge difference to millions of people around the globe. Thanks to his visionary approach to design, he revolutionized the music industry, personal computing, telephones, and tablet computers. He had an impact on millions of people, demonstrated by the outpouring of grief at the news of his death.

Not all companies can be Apple. But you should evaluate your company and ask yourself, who do we touch, and how big a difference do we make? From that basis, you can build confidence in your company.

Finally, you have to have confidence in what you're selling. This is pretty much the line in the sand for salespeople. If you don't believe in the service you're selling, why on earth should the client do so?

I've watched salespeople cold-call during training exercises when they clearly didn't believe in the value of what they were selling. When it came to presenting the benefits to the client, they were reading off a list. They weren't thinking, "Here's how this solves a significant problem for the client." Instead, most of them were probably thinking, "I wonder how long this Schiffman guy's gonna make us keep doing these cold calls."

There are two factors that must come into believing in what you're selling:

1. You've got to know that service better than anyone. You've got to know what benefits you're providing to potential customers, what the risks are of signing up for your service, and how you'll go about taking care of emergencies or problems with the service you're providing, and you've got to be able to quantify all of the benefits of your service into specific dollar amounts. No one will ever buy a service if all you've got to say is, "My IT service will improve your internal communications." But they're much more likely to buy it if you say something like, "My IT service will improve the speed of your internal communications by 175

percent in the first month, and this will translate into a productivity benefit of $1,000 per employee per week."

2. You've got to make your selling customer-centric. This means that when evaluating what service you're selling, you figure out the benefits to the customer first. Sometimes, when I ask salespeople in my training sessions, "Why are you selling X?" the answer comes back, "To make our sales quota and make sure our company makes its monthly numbers." Wrong answer! You're selling X because it fixes a problem for the client. If it doesn't do that, no one wants it.

THE ENERGIZED CALLER

I want, if I may, to take myself as an example.

First, do I believe in myself? Yes. When I get up in the morning, I'm so filled with energy that there have been several complaints about it (mainly from my wife, who's not a morning person). I know what I'm going to do, where I'm going to go, who I'm going to see, and what I need to accomplish in order to keep moving. I know the number of cold calls I'll have to make in order to generate continuing leads. I know what follow-up calls I'll have to make and what e-mails I should send to turn those leads into prospects. I'm a great advocate of to-do lists because I think they help you stay positive by focusing you and breaking your day into achievable, manageable goals. When I cross off something from my to-do list, I feel a sense of accomplishment, and that keeps me going after the next item on the list.

Second, do I believe in my company? Well, my company is pretty much myself, since I no longer own DEI Sales. And yes, I believe in myself; we just established that. But when I was running DEI Sales, I could tell myself without any question I believed in the company. I think we provided an important service, training more than half a million sales professionals. Our work made people's lives better. It made salespeople more confident and better at their jobs, and it improved clients' businesses by selling them something they needed.

Finally, do I believe in what I'm selling—in my case, sales training? Yes, absolutely. Sales training isn't a panacea, but it's an essential component of any good business. If your salespeople don't know how to sell, sooner or later you'll pay a price. My sales training methods have been honed to razor sharpness over three and a half decades, and I know they work. The proof lies in the long swell of satisfied clients bobbing in my wake and in the billions of dollars generated as a result of that training.

If that's not confidence, I don't know what is.

CLIENT CHALLENGE: "WHY SHOULD I TRUST YOU?"

20

Perhaps there aren't many readers of this book who remember the presidential campaign of 1976. It was a difficult time for America. Two years before, Richard Nixon had resigned the presidency in disgrace. His first vice president, Spiro Agnew, was already out of office, having been caught taking bribes (in the White House, no less!), and Nixon was followed by his new VP, Gerald Ford. Ford was a former senator from Michigan whose most notable accomplishment up to that point had been serving on the Warren Commission, which investigated the assassination of President Kennedy.

The country was wracked by inflation as well as a crisis of confidence over the disastrous course of the Watergate scandal. To top things off, in 1975 America had lost the Vietnam War, as refugees frantically scrambled into a helicopter atop the roof of the U.S. embassy in Saigon.

In short, it wasn't a very happy time.

Ford was opposed in the election by the governor of Georgia, Jimmy Carter. The two things everyone knew about Carter were that he was a peanut farmer and that he had a big, toothy smile. As far as a theme for his campaign, it came down to this:

"Trust me."

Today, when we're a lot more cynical about candidates from both political parties, it may seem astonishing to you that anyone won an election on that theme. But at a time when America seemed sick in its soul, that idea of trust appealed to a lot of people. Carter won the election. I'll leave you to judge the success or failure of his presidency. (I have fairly strong opinions on the subject, as I do on most things, but I'll keep them to myself.)

HOW TRUST IS BUILT OR DESTROYED

What I want to point out is that this election showed the power of trust when it's injected into a conversation at the right point. There are a couple of things to keep in mind:

1. Trust is largely built on experience. People trust other people to behave more or less the way they've done in the past. It's very difficult to trust a stranger because we've got no foundation to understand his future actions. Of course, you could argue that the story of Jimmy Carter's election contradicts this idea. The American people had no experience of Carter as a national leader. But this leads me to my second point.

2. Someone will extend trust to the degree that she needs something. The more she needs it, the more willing she is to trust someone to deliver it. In other words, when her need outweighs her natural caution, she's prepared to take more of a chance.

   In 1976, the American people were desperately in need of some positive leadership. They were willing to bet their future for the next four years on the relatively unknown Georgia governor. And there's an additional point.

3. Distrust is always stronger than trust. In other words, if someone has a reason to distrust you, that will tend to weigh heavier than actions you take to earn her trust. Broadly speaking, in my experience distrust outweighs trust by a factor of two to one. Harking back to our example, Ford's association with the discredited Nixon administration (and the fact that he'd granted Nixon a pardon after the president's resignation) meant that people tended to distrust him. He had to work harder to rebuild that trust, and in the end, he didn't succeed. Finally, there's this thought.

4. Even when trust is earned, it can be easily shattered. It took four years for Jimmy Carter to squander every bit of trust he'd built up during the election. In 1980, buffeted by the failed attempt to rescue hostages being held in Iran and a struggling economy, he was ousted from the presidency by Ronald Reagan.

HOW TRUST CAN BE DAMAGED IN A SALES CALL

Keeping these four points in mind, let's consider the following conversation between Al, a salesperson for a cleaning service, and James, a prospective customer who owns a computer hardware repair business.

Al: So we'll come in every other day after hours and do routine maintenance tasks on the shop floor as well as cleaning the kitchen and bathroom areas.

James: One thing that's of concern to me, Al. I know your staff has experience cleaning, but because we deal in computer hardware, some areas of the shop need special attention.

Al: Sure, sure, that's no problem, trust me. Now, what I'd like to turn to is our sliding scale of rates—

James: Excuse me, but I think we need to stay with this issue for a few minutes. The machines we work on are highly sensitive to dust and pollutants of various kinds, including fumes created by some kinds of cleaning solutions.

Al: Well, just send us a list of what solutions not to use, and we won't use them. Trust me, we know what we're doing.

James: Really? Have you serviced this kind of a plant before? One that deals in computer hardware?

Al: No, but I think cleaning routines are pretty much the same, no matter what stuff the company works on.

James: Do you know the accepted protocols for working around disassembled computers?

Al: I'm sure we've got those back at the company. Trust me, we pretty much cover all the bases when we're setting up a job.

James: Can you send me a list of former clients and any testimonials from them? I'd like to make sure you really are aware of all the ramifications of dealing with our sort of product. We've had that list from the two other companies we interviewed about this contract.

Al: Absolutely we are, James. You're really going to have to trust me on this.

James: Really, Al? Why should I trust you?

You can see where this is going. I predict that if the current trajectory of this conversation continues uninterrupted, we'll be looking at a blown sale of Carteresque proportions. Al seems to be under the impression that all he has to do is keep saying "Trust me," and everything will be okay. He's failing to see that Rule 2 in the preceding list is at work here: James doesn't need his services that badly—there are two other companies bidding on this contract. The burden is on Al to prove that his company is trustworthy when it comes to handling the special situation existing in James's shop. Of course, Al's also in the position of not being able to point James toward past experience with Al's company, so this means there's a problem with Rule 1. Trust is built on experience, but James doesn't have any experience of Al's service to go on.

One of the unfortunate things about the way Al handles the whole situation, trying to brush James's concerns under the carpet, is that it magnifies James's burgeoning distrust of him. Remember Rule 3? Al will have to work twice as hard to gain James's trust once he's lost it—and he has.

Al hasn't quite broken Rule 4 yet, but only because James isn't going to give him the chance. Since Al resists something as basic as providing a list of previous clients, James will run a mile to avoid working with him. And he's quite right to do so.

As a rule, I'm a trusting, easygoing sort of guy (though many of my acquaintances might offer a significantly different opinion). A couple of years ago, walking through Manhattan on my way to a meeting, I stopped at a bagel cart along the street and purchased a bagel.

Nothing unusual. The sort of thing that happens every day in New York—millions of times, probably. But when I bit into the bagel, it was so stale I almost broke my teeth. It tasted like something left over from two days before.

By this time I was a block and a half from the stand where I'd bought it, and I was in danger of being late to my meeting, so I didn't go back and complain. Instead, I simply never bought another bagel from that stand. The seller had lost my trust. Not a huge issue for him, considering all the bagels he sold daily, but if more and more of his customers started to feel that way, amid the cutthroat competition that exists among Manhattan's food carts, he'd be finished. In the same way, if Al loses the trust of more and more prospects (who'll tell other prospects), it won't be long before his company ceases to exist.

HOW TO WIN CLIENTS' TRUST

Rather than this unhappy ending, let's see how the conversation might have gone.

Al: So we'll come in every other day after hours and do routine maintenance tasks on the shop floor as well as cleaning the kitchen and bathroom areas.

James: One thing that's of concern to me, Al. I know your staff has experience cleaning, but because we deal in computer hardware, some areas of the shop need special attention.

Al: Sure. I can see that would be important. Do you have a list of protocols you would like us to follow while working on the assembly areas of the shop?

James: Yes, we've drawn up some guidelines.

Al: Great. What I'd like to do, if we win the bid on this contract, is ask someone from your company to come to our office and go over those protocols in detail with the people who'll be doing the cleaning so they understand exactly what should be done.

James: Yes, that would be a good idea, since there are certain specific procedures we'd need your people to follow.

Al: We've had some experience with this sort of situation before. If you'll look in the packet I gave you, on page 9 you'll find a list of our previous clients. On page 10 you'll find testimonials from them about the job we do. Looking at the list of clients, I think you can see several who are in similar businesses to you.

James: That raises a question in my mind about security and trade secrets.

Al: I'm glad you asked about that. It's a question of great importance to us. We require all of our staff to sign a nondisclosure agreement concerning those properties they work on. Any violation is grounds for immediate dismissal. I can say that we absolutely stand behind your concerns about the security of your property, whether it's physical or intellectual.

James: I'm glad you've addressed these concerns. I feel good about this.

Much better, right? Here's what happened:

1. Al didn't dismiss any of James's concerns. He spoke directly to them and made sure that each one was handled to James's satisfaction before moving on to another point.

2. He proposed specific solutions such as the nondisclosure agreement and the cleaning protocols.

3. He offered specific instances in which his company had performed a similar service at similar companies. In other words, keeping Rule 1 in mind, he built up for James a track record of experience.

4. He stressed that James's concerns are valid and of equal concern to his company. To that end, the company has built solutions for them.

The result, not surprisingly, is that James seems very confident that he can trust Al's company to do what it promises. Because remember, selling a service is selling a promise. And the foundation of that promise is trust.

YOUR RESPONSIBILITY TO YOUR CLIENT

21

arlier I said that one of the central components of my sales philosophy is that it's client-centric. That is, in everything you do as a salesperson, you should be asking yourself, "How's this going to help my client solve his or her problem?"

That said, of course, you're also in business to make money; if the client proposes terms unfavorable to you, you're under no obligation to accept them in the interest of making him happy. What concerns me more is that many salespeople, especially those who sell services, seem to have a hard time delineating the boundaries between their interests and those of their clients. In this chapter, I want to put forward some ideas on what those boundaries should be.

HONESTY

Let's start with one of the most basic aspects of your relationship to the client: honesty and integrity.

Cast your mind back some years ago to when the newspaper and television headlines were all about Enron. To briefly refresh your memory, Enron was a Houston-based energy company with many significant connections to the presidential administration of George W. Bush. The company was named one of the most innovative firms in the United States for several years running by *Forbes* magazine. Its books showed that it possessed enormous assets and profits, running into the billions of dollars.

The only problem was that it was all fraudulent. Company officials artificially inflated their assets, creating a series of limited liability companies that had no actual existence. Debits were moved to offshore companies so Enron could show a profit, pushing up its stock price and enriching its principal stockholders. In late 2001, the fraud was exposed and the house of cards collapsed. Several leaders of the company went to jail, and thousands of employees worldwide lost their jobs. Investors in the company lost millions of dollars.

Arthur Andersen, one of the country's most prominent accounting companies, was shown to have been complicit in the fraud. Further, Andersen employees attempted to cover their tracks by destroying thousands of documents and deleting e-mails that showed they knew Enron's profits weren't real. Andersen's conviction on charges of fraud was later overturned, but the company stopped doing audits. Another consequence of the scandal was the implementation of the Sarbanes-Oxley Act, designed to create greater accountability in corporate bookkeeping.

As a salesperson, I watched the scandal unfold with great interest and a certain amount of astonishment. I remember saying to friends and colleagues at the time, "Well, what did they expect? That they could keep this con going forever? Sooner or later it was going to collapse." The lesson for anyone selling services is clear: Your service rests on your integrity as a company. This is especially true if you deal in things such as accounting and bookkeeping, but it's really just as valid if you're selling lawnmower servicing. Your clients are taking your word that you'll do a good job and be honest with them about what's wrong or right about whatever it is you're servicing.

Some years ago, my daughter bought a secondhand car. She bought it from a dealer I'd dealt with before, someone I trusted. She was a bit suspicious when, as she was getting ready to take the vehicle for a test drive, she had some trouble starting it, but the dealer assured her it just needed a new battery and he'd put one in before the purchase was completed.

Well, that was a mistake. The car, I regret to say, was a complete lemon. It constantly needed maintenance, broke down with such regularity that you could practically set your calendar by it, and cost an armful in parts and service. After a year or so of struggling with it, my daughter bought a new car—from a different dealer, needless to say. Since I'd given her the original recommendation, I pitched in and paid part of the cost of the new car.

Just as was the case with Enron, the car dealer was attempting to get by the rules with a little sleight of hand. And just as was the case with Enron, it backfired—I spread the word among all my friends that as far as I was concerned, this car dealer was dishonest and couldn't be counted on to sell a skateboard, let alone a car.

So this is my First Rule of Responsibility Toward Clients: You must be honest with them. You must believe in what you're selling to your clients, as I discussed in a previous chapter, but at the same time you can't make promises you've no intention of keeping. Nor can you exaggerate the benefits of your service. If you do, you may make the sale, but in the long run you won't keep the client. And you'll find that an angry former client can do irreparable harm to your business.

SERVICE PROBLEM

Okay, so you've been completely honest with your client. You've sold him a service, and then he calls up with a problem. Here's where your second set of responsibilities kicks in.

On occasion I've seen salespeople who were great with client relations right up to the moment that the ink was dry on the contracts. Then they disappeared.

Some years ago, my wife and I had dinner at a restaurant in Manhattan. It had come highly recommended, and we were looking forward to a pleasant evening. We were seated, and the waitress took our drink order, brought us our drinks, and gave us a few minutes to linger over our choices for dinner.

The few minutes went on a little longer . . . then a little longer . . . and then I was starting to get mad. Our drinks were finished, and we hadn't even put in our requests for the meal. I flagged down the hostess and explained the problem to her; she graciously took the order herself and walked it back to the kitchen. When she brought the meal to us, along with a couple of complimentary glasses of wine, I asked about the original waitress.

"Oh," said the hostess with a short bark of laughter, "she does that all the time. We call her 'the gray ghost.'"

Some salespeople are gray ghosts. They start off well, but somehow they think that once the contract is signed, they don't need to think about the client until the next time comes to make a sale.

Wrong, wrong, wrong!

When a client calls you up with a problem, you need to do the following things:

1. Apologize for the inconvenience. It doesn't matter that you haven't determined how the problem arose or whether it's really your fault. Apologize anyway. It makes it clear to the client that you're sympathetic to him and not adversarial.

2. Ask for a detailed description of the problem. Throughout, listen actively to what's being said. (For a refresher course on active listening, go back and reread Chapter 15.)

3. Chances are you'll need to refer the client to a different part of your organization. That's fine, but when possible, give him a name as well as a department that he needs to speak to. That makes the whole transaction personal.

4. If at all possible—and in this age of complex electronic communication, it usually is possible—transfer his call to the right department and stay on the line until the person at the other end comes on. Make a brief introduction. ("Suzanne? This is Jack in sales. I have Mr. Smith on the line from the ABC Corporation. He's got a problem with his IT service and would like to speak to you. Jack? This is Suzanne. She'll be able to assist you.") Only then should you hang up the phone.

5. Follow through. Even if you're confident that the problem has been solved, even if Suzanne comes up to you in the hallway and tells you that she was able to solve it, call the client back and make sure he was happy with the service he received. Some people might argue that this isn't part of a salesperson's job. I'd say it's an essential part of the job. The person who called is your client. You want to make sure he stays your client.

So the second element of your responsibility to your client is to give good service, be attentive and helpful, and make sure he stays happy.

RESPONSIBLE COMMUNICATION

The third part of this formula of responsibility is to be communicative. This isn't difficult, but it can be time-consuming, which is why some salespeople are inclined to skimp on it. That's a dangerous thing to do, though.

When I was very young (that is to say, about 20), I had a holiday job working in the shirts department of a big retailer. It was one of my first experiences with sales, and I have to say that at the time I didn't like it much. The customers were rude (well, it was Christmas, so pretty much everyone was rude), and the permanent salespeople hated the holiday help because they felt (rightly) that we were taking sales away from them. But one of the salespeople, in a moment of civility, talked to me for a bit about his job.

"Every week," he said, "I sit down on Saturday or Sunday night and make a list of upcoming sale items. I scan the newspaper for information about special events that I think my best customers might be interested in and for which they might want to get some new clothes. Then I call the customers and talk to them about those things, let them know what sales we've got coming up, and so on. That way, I keep them coming back to me. When I'm not at the counter, they ask for me, and they won't buy things from anyone else."

This was a revelation to me. I'd always assumed that salespeople just stood behind the counter and rang up purchases. I never really thought about the proactive work that goes into building a customer base. I don't say that this conversation turned me in the direction of a career in sales, but it undoubtedly contributed to it.

When you're selling a service, you need to stay in regular contact with the customer. You need to find out how the service is working and if there's anything you can do to improve it. You need to find out the bugs in the service so they can be corrected. And you need to make yourself available for anything the client wants to talk about. That way you stress the essential relationship you want to build with the client: a partnership, in which both of you benefit from the sale of your service.

I can't overemphasize the importance of the regular check-in phone call or e-mail. It doesn't have to be long, but it's important that it be regular. That way you stress to the client your reliability and your willingness to listen to any problems.

These three elements—honesty, service, and communication—are the foundation of a good relationship with your client. Keep them at the forefront of your activity, and you'll build and maintain a client base that will last a professional lifetime.

CLIENT CHALLENGE: "SOMEONE ELSE CAN DO IT BETTER!"

Q uestion: How many actors does it take to screw in a lightbulb? Answer: A hundred and one. One to screw it in, and a hundred to say, "I could have done it better."

I remember hearing that joke back in my much younger days when I was involved in theater. It's the sort of self-deprecating pleasantry that aspiring actors toss around to keep themselves grounded in some sort of reality. I still think it's funny, especially when you put it against the self-important, ego-inflating nonsense that some actors spout in the pages of popular magazines and on talk shows. Besides, the joke represents a measure of reality. There are practically no activities you can engage in that someone, somewhere, doesn't think he or she could do better.

In my time as a sales trainer, I've run into this line of thought on a number of occasions. One instance leaps to mind. It was about 10 or 12 years ago, and I had signed up to do a training session for the sales force of a new company, part of the dot-com boom that we were then experiencing. I was a little surprised, truth to tell, that I'd been asked to do the session at all, because most of the dot-coms I knew of didn't think their salespeople needed any training. They were the smartest guys in the room, the masters of the universe. What did they need training for?

But this particular company had called me in, so I did what I usually do—I had a couple of sessions with the salespeople, talking to them about what they were doing. I listened to them make cold calls. And I ran through some scenarios with them, asking them to sell me or sell each other their company's product.

During our last session, the CEO of the company walked into the room and stood at the back. He was, along with much of the rest of his workforce, wearing blue jeans and a T-shirt that had the name of a band on it. His hair was tousled, and he didn't look a day over 14. Yet this was the man running a company with millions in invested venture capital.

The session was a question-and-answer one, with the sales folks tossing out questions. I've found over the years that the best way to handle such sessions is with a very light hand. Often, if you allow questions to get batted back and forth between the people in the group, they'll often answer themselves. So I tried to say as little as possible. After the session, the CEO came up to me.

"Thanks, Steve," he said. "But I wonder if you were really very involved in that."

I started to explain, but he cut me short. He was obviously someone who had much more important things to do than stand around talking to me. "I just think that if we're paying the kind of money we paid you to come in and train people, you ought to train them," he said. "I mean, I could have done what you just did. Better, in fact, since I know our product a lot better than you."

I had to clamp my teeth down hard to keep from losing it. "I think," I said, speaking slowly and carefully, "that before you say something like that you ought to wait until you see the results of my training. Give these people six months and compare their numbers to what you were seeing before. Then you can tell me I didn't train them."

He shrugged and walked off. As a matter of fact, his numbers did improve, and I believe that a substantial amount of that was directly due to my training. It didn't help him, ultimately, and his company went the way of most of the dot-coms—busted when it became clear that they had no viable product. All of their venture capital dried up and blew away. I was sad because I never like to see a former client go under, though there was a tiny whisper of *Schadenfreude* (a German word that means, essentially, taking pleasure in the misfortunes of other people) in my soul. At the same time, I hoped that the salespeople I had trained would go out and find other jobs and that they'd take with them some of the training I had given them.

SELLING TO DOMINANT CLIENTS

The point here is that when you're selling a service you're going to confront people who think they already know how to do what you're proposing to do. And they think they can do it better. Let's look at a salesperson who's encountered exactly this situation: Lou, who's selling a laundry service to Alice, owner of a chain of restaurants.

Alice: Lou, I appreciate your coming in here to make this pitch, but frankly it seems to me that we could easily do what you're doing by installing a washer and dryer at each of our locations. I mean that's really all you do, isn't it? You would just be washing our uniforms and dish towels and aprons. So why couldn't we do that ourselves?

Lou: Well, I think you're not seeing—

Alice: I mean it would be more efficient to have those facilities right on site rather than having time wasted bringing the stuff back and forth from your shop to all our stores, right?

Lou: It really wouldn't take that long. See, we're centrally located and—

Alice: I think we could just integrate this into each shift's duties. When the shift comes off, they'd toss their uniforms and aprons into a bin next to the washer. The next shift, when they come on, just throws that load into the machine and starts it up.

Lou: It's really not that simple. You're losing a lot of efficiencies by not having it done by a service.

Alice: What kind of efficiencies? Can you give me some specific facts and figures here, Lou?

Lou: Well, I can work up something for my next visit.

Alice: You mean you don't have anything for me now? Didn't you anticipate this? Didn't you think I was going to ask these kinds of questions?

Lou: No, I mean . . . I—

Alice: Lou, I'm concerned about how serious this bid is. There's no reason I can see why we couldn't do this better. And since you haven't given this the kind of attention it deserves, I don't see why we need to continue with this meeting. I've got dinner shift coming up, and I don't have time to waste.

And there goes Lou out the door with his tail between his legs. Sad, but inevitable, given the dynamics of the conversation. Actually, it's hardly fair to call it a conversation. Lou barely got in a word edgewise before Alice interrupted him.

Everyone, sooner or later, sells to someone like Alice. That's because she represents a basic type of personality. I've talked before in my books about various kinds of personalities and how to sell to them (see *The 25 Toughest Sales Objections* and *The Power of Positive Selling*). Alice is what I've characterized as a Dominant.

HOW TO SELL TO A DOMINANT CLIENT

Dominants are, well, just that: dominant. They want to throw you off your game by interrupting you with questions, demands for information, and challenges. To some degree they do this as a negotiating tactic; after all, if they can keep you wrong-footed, when they do decide to make a deal it'll probably be more advantageous to them. But at the same time, they do this as a basic extension of their personality. Dominants are people who are convinced they know what's best and how to do things better than anyone. Their challenges to you are a way of expressing that. They're particularly challenging when selling services because what you're selling seems abstract—something whose benefits will be realized, often, some distance into the future. This allows Dominants to play the role of someone rooted in the here and now. They don't want fancy promises; they want guarantees of specific results, and if you can't give them, they want nothing more to do with you.

Selling services to Dominants isn't a matter of out-shouting them. Shouting, as I've said elsewhere, can be a useful sales tactic, but usually not when you're dealing with Dominants. In those cases, the call turns into a shouting match and then explodes, leaving wreckage behind. Rather, you need to focus on facts and figures. Be firm and don't be afraid to assert yourself—without, of course, being rude. Knowing that you're going to be selling to a Dominant (and a crucial part of your research should be to try to learn as much as possible about the personality of who you're selling to) should motivate you to be especially detailed in preparing your pitch.

With this in mind, listen to version two of that conversation.

Alice: Lou, I appreciate your coming in here to make this pitch, but frankly it seems to me that we could easily do what you're doing by installing a washer and dryer at each of our locations.

I mean that's really all you do, isn't it? You would just be washing our uniforms and dish towels and aprons. So why couldn't we do that ourselves?

Lou: Let me ask you, Alice—on average, what's the hourly wage of your employees?

Alice: I don't have the exact number in front of me, but I'd guess it's around $15 to $20 an hour.

Lou: Okay, now in addition to washing your uniforms, you're going to need them pressed when they come out of the dryer, right?

Alice: Yes. What's your point?

Lou: And there may be stains that will have to be specially treated, since you're working with food.

Alice: Okay.

Lou: The average restaurant of your size generates six loads of laundry per day, assuming a lunch shift and a dinner shift. That includes uniforms for the entire staff, dishcloths, napkins, and tablecloths. Each load, including washing and drying time, takes an average of 90 minutes. So every day, each of your restaurants is creating laundry that takes 360 minutes, or six hours of washing and drying time.

Alice: Okay.

Lou: If we add into that an additional two hours to deal with stains and special problems—which we've found is pretty much the average for this sort of thing—we're looking at a total of eight hours of laundry time. Do you really need almost $1,000 per week of staff time taken up with something that you can do through our service for $600 per week?

Alice: Probably not. I see where you're going with this.

Lou: As well, I know space is precious in any restaurant. You'd be losing at least 100 square feet to washers and dryers. A service like ours is the perfect answer for you. It takes an ongoing problem and makes it go away.

Alice: All right, let's talk terms.

Truth to tell, I doubt Alice was ever very serious about installing washers and dryers in all of her restaurants, but in the first conversation she used this as a pushing point against Lou. In the second conversation, Lou did what any good salesperson should do when confronted with a Dominant personality. He overwhelmed her with facts. He proved that he'd thought about her situation, that he wanted to solve her problem and was willing to work with her to do it. She still has an aggressive edge to her personality, and she'll assert it again when they negotiate the exact terms of the contract. But she'll do so from a place of increased respect for Lou. And he's gotten her past her conviction that she can perform the service he's selling better than he can.

BUILDING
YOUR BRAND

23

Let me tell you a story. A story about motorcycles.

Specifically, about Harley-Davidson. It's a very instructive little tale. Harley got started in the early twentieth century, but it wasn't until World War I that it really took off. The military demand for motorcycles meant the company kicked into high gear (so to speak!), and it ramped up production. Much the same thing happened on a larger scale during World War II; Harley, which was one of only two motorcycle companies to survive the Great Depression, was in huge demand by the U.S. military.

Then came peace. During the 1950s, Harley continued to dominate the U.S. market. But in the 1960s, demand fell sharply. The company slashed its workforce, but in the face of fierce competition from Japanese companies such as Kawasaki and Nissan, Harley struggled. Its market share dropped dramatically, and there was talk of declaring bankruptcy.

The problem was that compared to the Japanese bikes that were flooding the U.S. market, the Harley machine was inferior in almost every significant way: handling, speed, reliability. Harley owners complained that they spent more time fixing their bikes than riding them.

Harley-Davidson's leaders took a long, hard look at their company. They examined the history of the company and its manufacturing practices. And then they carried out one of the most effective and famous rebranding campaigns in American business history.

They reasoned that they couldn't compete with the Japanese on issues of quality. Japanese bikes were just better; that was all there was to it. But if that was the case, what could they sell Harleys on? They concluded that people bought Harleys not for performance but for image.

It was a revelation.

Harley riders, inspired by Peter Fonda's character, Captain America, in the film *Easy Rider,* saw themselves as outsiders. Knights of the road. This idea was also framed by biker gangs like the Hell's Angels and by movies like Marlon Brando's *The Wild One* ("What are you rebelling against, Johnny?" "Whaddya got?") At the same time, Harley buyers were older men, mostly white, mostly middle class (you had to have middle-class money to keep your motorcycle in decent repair).

With all this in mind, Harley's owners said, in effect, "We're not selling motorcycles as vehicles to get you from point A to point B. We're selling motorcycles as an image. An image of a rebel. We're selling toys to middle-class, older white guys."

With that branding in place, Harley carefully and patiently rebuilt itself. Today it holds a strong market share position, and it's become an iconic American brand, as embedded in our national consciousness as Popsicles and Kleenex.

Before you ask, I should tell you that I've never ridden a Harley or any other motorcycle and have no intention of doing so. I know my limitations, and I respect them. That said, I'm a huge admirer of the Harley-Davidson company for its branding smarts.

THE BRAND MAKES THE PRODUCT

What is a brand? Essentially, it's a promise to the customer. The promise does not need to be about the actual qualities of the product or service. That's a very important distinction to make. In fact, many times the brand is about something far less tangible. It's about emotional experience more than actual experience.

Take Nike, one of the most recognizable brands in the world. What qualities do you identify with the famous swoosh? Probably speed, excitement, and talent—vaguely associated with Michael Jordan. This is what Nike promises you'll experience when you purchase a pair of its shoes. Not the actuality of these things, but the feeling, the promise of them.

If this sounds a bit confusing or deceptive to you, think of some other famous brands:

Burger King—fast food individualized to your taste ("Have it your way!")

Volvo—safe, reliable, slightly stodgy transportation

Apple—innovative, cutting-edge designed products

What I suggest to you is that along with your company brand, it's important to build your personal brand.

Now wait a minute, you might protest. I can see a company having a brand—for example, the Microsoft brand says the basic software you need to run any computer for any task—but how can an individual have a brand?

In fact, brand building is essential these days for anyone in business, nowhere more so than in sales. People have brands all the time. For instance (and I know I'm reaching back a bit into time for this one), remember Walter Cronkite, the newsman? He was, at one time, one of the most famous people in America. The reason? Because he projected a fatherly image: comforting, reliable, authoritative. He brought us news of some of the greatest events of the 1960s and 1970s, including the deaths of President Kennedy, Martin Luther King Jr., and Bobby Kennedy; the end of the Vietnam War; and the resignation of President Nixon. People listened to him because his personal brand projected a promise of objective, fair, authoritative reporting.

HOW TO BUILD YOUR PERSONAL BRAND

So if you're going to build a personal brand, what should it consist of? Well, first, since you're in sales, you want to be seen as reliable. That means that in your dealings with other people, you do what they expect you to do. If you make a promise, you keep it. If you say you're going to call a client on the 25th at 3:30 in the afternoon, that's when you make the phone call. In other words, you project a brand image that says to clients and prospects, "If this person promises me something, I know it's going to get done. That's someone I want to do business with."

A second component of your brand is honesty. I've talked about this in other chapters, but I keep stressing it because when you're selling a service it's so important that you not overpromise what the service can deliver and that you be straightforward about what you're selling. If you do this and do it consistently, people will start to say, "Man, when Sheila told me that her IT company could increase my storage capacity by 50 percent, she wasn't kidding!" In these situations, it's best if you slightly underpromise so you can exceed expectations. Whatever the case, concentrate on delivering what you've said you'll deliver, and people will respect you.

Third, deliver respect. Remember that Aretha Franklin song? "R-E-S-P-E-C-T. Find out what it means to me." That's what your clients are telling you. They want you to respect what they're doing, their opinions, and their wishes. You can disagree with them, of course, but remember that they're the ones with their profits on the line, and they're depending on you to deliver the goods so their business will continue to grow. If a salesperson consistently projects an attitude that his clients are a bunch of yo-yos who don't know enough to come in from the rain, you can be sure that those clients are going to find somewhere else to go very quickly.

HOW TO PROJECT YOUR BRAND

All right. You've got the elements of your personal brand down. Now how do you project them? I'm not—repeat, not—suggesting that branding means you've got to go out and get a personal logo or something. In some cases, it's helpful to use a tagline that you can put on your business cards. For instance, I'm generally called America's Number One Corporate Sales Trainer. That's the brand image I want to project—someone with a lot of experience in training salespeople, someone who's widely respected in his field.

For you, as a service salesperson, projecting your brand will be something more subtle. You need to integrate the elements of your brand into the way you craft your sales pitches, the way you interact with clients, and the way in which you comport yourself in meetings. In other words, you have to live your brand.

This can be very challenging because a brand is something that is quite easy to damage. To take a corporate example, there was a time when McDonald's started offering salads and healthy alternatives at its stores. The move was a disaster, and McDonald's quickly pulled back from it. The reason? Well, no one goes into McDonald's because he or she expects to eat healthy food. McDonald's brand promise is food delivered fast—within a minute. Its offerings range from breakfast to lunch to snacks, but health is not a brand-significant component of its brand; nor should it be.

Borders Bookstore is another case of a brand that tried to do too much, to be everything to everyone. When the company began to spin out of control about five years ago, its top executives reacted by first trying to expand the number of book titles they were offering per store, then to expand the number of stores (including smaller stores, called Borders Express), and then to chase after their chief competitor, Barnes & Noble. What they didn't do was to successfully challenge Barnes & Noble in the area where this chain held an advantage: electronic books. B&N's Nook carved out a significant place in the e-book reader market, and Borders staggered from one crisis to the next until it collapsed, a tragic victim of bad management and bad branding.

Your personal brand needs to concentrate on a small number of attributes—basically the ones discussed earlier—and you need to keep coming back to these in all your discussions with clients. When pitching to new prospects, when cold-calling, talk about what you've delivered in the past. Explain, using specific facts and figures, how much your service has improved other companies' performance. Stress the value of easy access to you and explain that you want to work with the client on a long-term basis.

That's the best possible way to project your personal brand.

Harley-Davidson is a great example of a company that turned its brand around and refocused it in a direction that made the company profitable. The owners of the company had the sense to see where their competitive advantage lay—they made a machine that was great for people who had the time and money to spend their weekends tinkering with the bikes as well as riding them. In the same way, you emphasize and develop your personal brand by asking, "What do I do better than my competitors? Why is what I'm selling better than the other guy's offering?" Finding a significant competitive advantage is a huge breakthrough that can lead to substantial sales and an increased commission for you.

And who knows? With that sudden windfall in your paycheck, you might want to go out and get a Harley.

CLIENT CHALLENGE: "WE'RE GIVING UP TOO MUCH CONTROL"

24

Some years ago, in the company of my children, I went to Disneyland in California.

I'm not big on theme parks, and after this experience I haven't changed my opinion. Disneyland, to me, felt oddly like being thrust back into a sort of idealized 1950s—it wasn't reality, just a simulation of it. But it's definitely a place for kids. We were surrounded by hordes of them, chattering, laughing, and shrieking.

We decided to try a couple of the rides. These included—naturally—some of the roller coasters. The first one we got on, Thunder Mountain, took us slowly up the first hill. Then we plunged down into a tunnel, spun right with a shriek of metal on metal, and sailed back into daylight before swinging around another hairpin curve. The ride lasted about eight or nine minutes, and I was laughing and shouting with the rest of the kids on the ride. I came off with a feeling of exhilaration. "Let's do another one!" I exclaimed. My wife looked at me as if I were crazy.

"No, no!" I said. "That was fun. Let's do another." So we picked another at random. Space Mountain.

We stood in line for what seemed about an hour. Finally we got into the cars, strapped ourselves in, and began the ride. We went up and up into utter blackness. Then, suddenly, it felt as if the bottom of my stomach dropped out.

Around me in the blackness I could see faint glows of "stars"and "planets." My ears were filled with the sound of someone screaming—a moment later I realized it was me. It was one of the most terrifying experiences of my life. When the ride came to a halt, I climbed out, my shirt clinging to my back and my hands trembling. Space Mountain pretty well cured me of any desire to ever again ride a roller coaster. (I should, in fairness, point out that there are a lot of people who *love* Space Mountain. If you're one of them, I apologize for my wimpiness.)

Thinking about the experience afterward, I concluded that the thing that made Space Mountain scary, as opposed to Thunder Mountain, was the fact that I couldn't see where we were going except right before we got there. As a result, I felt completely out of control. I knew, of course, that the ride had been safety tested, but that didn't prevent me from imagining all the ways in which disaster could happen.

CLIENTS DON'T LIKE TO FEEL OUT OF CONTROL

I've found this to be a useful reference point whenever some prospect says to me, "I don't want to buy what you're selling because it would mean giving up too much control."

This objection is particularly prevalent among those who are considering buying services. There's a good reason for that. When a client buys a service, he's outsourcing some aspect of his business. It may be a relatively marginal element (for instance, cleaning) or one that's essential to the business's well-being (for example, accounting). Either way, he's giving up an element of control. Good service salespeople recognize this and accept it. The key to making the sale in that case is not to deny the basic fact of what your service does; it's in showing how the client can reassert some measure of control through your accountability.

Accountability is one of the most important aspects of selling a service. A service is an ongoing thing whose benefits become clear over time. If, at any point, the client feels these benefits are nonexistent, he's going to complain about it—and rightly so. You have to demonstrate that you're willing to fix what is wrong and explain anything he doesn't understand. In other words, you have to show that even though he's given up some control, he hasn't lost complete control. You have to give him a Thunder Mountain experience rather than a Space Mountain experience, to hark back to my metaphor.

With that in mind, let's see what happens when George, a salesperson for an accounting firm, is talking to Steven, the CFO for a midlevel corporation.

Steve: Can you give me an idea of exactly what is included in your accounting service?

George: Sure. We handle all day-to-day operations, including inflow and outflow, tracking of all expenditures and income. We deal with all vendors as well as handling employee payroll, tax preparation, Sarbanes-Oxley compliance—

Steve: Wait, wait. I'm a little uncomfortable with placing all of our financial operations in the hands of an outside company. What I'm looking for is just someone who can handle the payroll and benefit aspects of what we do.

George: I understand that, but I think you really would benefit much more from a total package. That way we can better evaluate how your business is running and can make better recommendations to you about your corporate strategy.

Steve: It sounds, from what you're saying, as if you wouldn't so much be a service as a corporate partner.

George: Well, that's probably a good way to look at it. We'd be your partners.

Steve: But that's not really what I'm looking for right now. We don't want a partner, we want someone who can handle an aspect of our business that takes up too much of our time at the moment.

George: But you can't isolate the questions of payroll and benefits from everything else you do. It's all part of the financial performance of your company. You can only make decisions about rightsizing your workforce and adjusting your benefits package if you know how the rest of the company's functioning.

Steve: That's right. But to be clear: we make those decisions, not some third party.

George: Well, I think you've overlooking a really significant benefit that our total financial services package can bring to you.

Steve: That may be the case, but we're not willing to give up that much control right now. Or ever. Thanks for coming in. We'll let you know our final decision in a couple of weeks.

I'm pretty sure I know what that final decision is going to be, don't you? And it's not going to be one George will be happy about.

WHAT MAKES CLIENTS FEARFUL OF LOSING CONTROL

Here's what George did wrong:

1. **He tried to sell too much.** It was clear from the beginning of the conversation—and probably even before the

portion that we listened in on—that Steve had a much more limited set of services in mind. George, seeing the possibility of a larger sale and larger commission, pushed for a broader package. As a result, he's probably going to come away with nothing, as well as a prospect who's unlikely to buy from him in the future. It would have been better to make the smaller sale and use it to build the relationship with Steve's company. A big sale usually has a lot of experience and trust as its foundation. George needs to be patient and build that trust.

2. **He argued with the prospect.** I'm strongly opposed to arguing during a sales call. It doesn't get you anywhere because the prospect can always win the argument by simply bringing the call to a close. Instead, you have to get a feeling for where the prospect wants to go and go along with him. That doesn't mean that you give up direction of the conversation; it simply means you don't act as a roadblock. Through creative questioning and nudging, you can bring the sale to where you want it, helping the client in that direction.

    An editor I know once told me, "The job of an editor is to help the author tell the story he wants to tell." I think that applies to sales as well. The job of a salesperson is to help the client do what he wants to do.

3. **He didn't pick up on the client's comfort level.** That's key when selling services. If the client becomes uncomfortable with losing too much control, you need to dial things back. Find out how much he's willing to cede to the service you're selling. Then adjust. A lot of George's instincts here are good ones—it's true that he wants to paint a picture of his company partnering with Steve's for their mutual benefit. The problem is that Steve isn't comfort-

able with that level of relationship yet. In this respect selling is like dating. It only works if both parties involved are comfortable with how fast things are going.

REASSURE CLIENTS BY DEMONSTRATING YOUR ACCOUNTABILITY

Okay, let's go back to George and Steve again and see if George has learned anything.

Steve: Can you give me an idea of exactly what is included in your accounting service?

George: Sure. We handle all day-to-day operations, including inflow and outflow, tracking of all expenditures and income. We deal with all vendors as well as handling employee payroll, tax preparation, Sarbanes-Oxley compliance—

Steve: Wait, wait. I'm a little uncomfortable with placing all of our financial operations in the hands of an outside company. What I'm looking for is just someone who can handle the payroll and benefit aspects of what we do.

George: I see. Well, let's talk specifically about that. What do you see an accounting service doing in relationship to payroll and benefits?

Steve: I'd like to see them maintain all records, cut checks, and keep track of benefits, add and remove employees as needed, and help us deal with issues like payroll taxes.

George: I see. This would be for all employees, including those at the executive level?

Steve: Yes. Everyone.

George: Okay. What I'd like to show you is this website, maintained by our company. I have a sample page here that shows what we do. If you sign a contract with us, all your employees will have access to this site, where they can track all their benefits, including PTO, medical, insurance, and so forth. As CFO, you also have access to all records on the site, so you can make sure everything's working the way you want.

Steve: What about checks?

George: We would cut all payroll checks, but you would have final approval each pay period over the amount paid out. We would also flag anything unusual and bring it to your attention. That way we minimize any surprises for you.

Steve: Good. Who maintains the site?

George: We do all maintenance.

Steve: And what happens if the site goes down?

George: We've got sufficient backup in place that we're confident that won't happen. If anything happens, though, we have full backup of the records on our servers so nothing will be lost. Furthermore, at the end of every four-month period we send you a detailed accounting of your company's payroll and benefits performance so you can track how you're doing against your company goals. We will customize that accounting to your internal goals, working with you to make sure you're getting the information you need.

Steve: Okay, and about security?

George: Let's go over the security protocols in place. I also have comments here from some of our other clients that you may want to take a look at concerning both security and record keeping. I think you'll find they've been very satisfied with the services we provide.

George has gotten back on track. Right away in the conversation he sees the direction Steve wants to go. He accepts that the sale is going to be for limited services, but that's fine. There'll be more opportunities for other sales down the road. Right now he needs to reassure Steve that even though he's putting his payroll in someone else's hands, Steve's company still maintains a measure of control over it. He's not going to be riding a roller coaster in the dark; instead, he's going to be watching where he's going every bit of the way.

That's the kind of thing that makes clients feel comfortable.

CREATING CLIENT CONFIDENCE

25

It doesn't seem that long ago that a young, naive salesman sat in a conference room, thumbing through the papers in his briefcase, waiting for his first sales call to start. He could feel his palms sweating, and he pulled out a handkerchief from his pocket and touched it to his forehead. Ten in the morning, and his stomach felt empty. He could sense a rumble from his midsection that sounded like a volcanic eruption.

The door opened, and the client walked in. The salesman stood up and shook hands, conscious of the fact that his shirt was sticking to his back and his clothes felt two or three sizes too large. Too large, hell! He was waddling in his suit. Who picked this thing out, anyway?

And why was his mouth so dry? It felt like the Sahara Desert. He couldn't remember the last time he'd had a drink of water. What was it? Two, three weeks? A month? He cleared his throat, and the rasp could be heard in Johannesburg.

Time to start the pitch. He fumbled in the briefcase. Where were the damn papers? He had them just a minute ago. Wait a minute . . . maybe his secretary had forgotten to pack them. Maybe he'd dropped them on the way in. Maybe he'd left them in the cab, where he'd been intently studying them on the way to the call.

Well, I won't torment you any longer with this. The salesman was me, of course. And although time may have magnified a few of the details, that's pretty much what I felt like on my first sales call. In fact, I wouldn't be surprised if you felt the same way. Unless you're an unusual kind of salesperson, most of the time we feel on our first call as if everything can, will, and does go wrong.

The value of experience is that it puts things in perspective. When you're the veteran of half a thousand sales calls, you've got the routine down. You know what you're going to say and what the client may reply. You've heard just about every conceivable response, and you've got your answers ready. You're poised, cool, and collected because you know from your long history in this business that there's nothing—literally nothing—the client can throw at you that you haven't seen before.

Now ask yourself: Which type of salesperson is more likely to inspire confidence in the client? Pretty obvious, isn't it?

The client-salesperson relationship is often an odd and occasionally a confusing one. I've tried over the years to figure it out:

- Sometimes it seems like a marriage: both of you want something, and you want somewhat different things, but cooperation gets you a lot closer to getting to your goal than competition. (That's one analysis of the dynamics of marriage. My wife has another, but we won't go into that now.)

- Sometimes it's like a contest: both of you are reaching for the same prize, and in the end only one of you is going to get it.

- Sometimes it's like trying to form a friendship with someone you don't know very well: you have to spend a lot of time getting to know one another before you're willing to let down your barriers and become trusting.

In truth, I think the sales relationship is all of these things and more. But one thing I do know about it: it's symbiotic. Both of you draw from one another and play off each other's moods. Nowhere is this truer than in the area of confidence.

Here's the basic proposition: If you have no confidence in yourself and what you're selling, neither will your client. The client will sense your lack of confidence in a hundred different ways:

- **How well you know what you're selling.** If you don't display an intimate knowledge of the service your company can provide, the client will assume the simplest explanation of that fact: the service isn't that good.

- **How much information you've gathered about the client.** The client doesn't want to spend the entire call explaining the basics of his business to you. He assumes that you've done some research. And if you can't bring it to the fore immediately, he'll lose respect for you.

- **How open you are to the client.** If you signal that you're just there to recite a canned sales pitch without any reference to the client's specific needs, he won't bother to spend 10 minutes with you.

CONFIDENCE INSPIRES CONFIDENCE

Above all, when pitching to a client you must exude confidence. You must demonstrate that you know what you're doing, you know about the client, and you've got the solutions to the client's specific problems. This is where building client confidence in your service begins.

There are, I think, several parts to this process.

First, you've got to have attitude. In some of my other books I've talked about the importance of attitude in sales. This is not to be confused with arrogance, which is an attitude that's taken a sharp left turn and gotten derailed. Arrogance means you've stopped listening to the client and are just listening to yourself. And if you're listening only to yourself, then you're just selling to yourself. Attitude, on the other hand, means self-confidence, a belief that you'll do what it takes to make the sale because you think that the service you're selling is the best possible solution for the client. Attitude, in other words, is client-based.

Second, you've got to have a genuine interest in what makes the client tick. You've got to spend the time asking questions about his business and demonstrate that you're listening to the answers, taking in the information, and processing it into a series of practical solutions.

Third, you've got to have the facts and figures to back up your claims about the service. Keep in mind that while a product will show results virtually at once, a service generally produces results over time. So your approach should always be historical. Tell the client, "Our IT service has produced an increase of 25 percent greater productivity among our clients, as measured over a two-year period." That last point is crucial, since you don't want to overpromise to the client; instead, you want to get him thinking about the long-term benefits of what you offer, to see how it fits into his plans for the future.

THE FIRST 20 SECONDS COUNT

Harking back to my description at the beginning of this chapter of my own miserable initiation into the world of sales, I want to stress the importance of some basics of body language as elements that contribute to building client confidence. The first 20 seconds or so of meeting a new client are probably among the most important time you'll ever spend with her. It's your chance to make an indelible first impression and to create an atmosphere of confidence on which you can safely build.

What should go into those 20 seconds? Here are 10 suggestions:

1. Before the client walks into the room, try to clean up any traces of sweat, either from your forehead or your hands. Sweat conveys nervousness and leads to an impression that you lack confidence in what you're selling.

2. Give a firm handshake. A "wet fish" handshake says you're weak and don't believe in yourself. An overly firm grip demonstrates an attempt to intimidate the client, and that won't go over any better.

3. Look the client in the face, without staring but without averting your eyes or avoiding any sort of eye contact. "Shifty-eye syndrome" shows the client that you're either trying to put something over on her or not really sure of the value of the service you're providing.

4. Your voice should be pitched to a comfortable listening level. Don't be ashamed to practice this on colleagues or family members. There's nothing worse than to go through a sales call shouting at the client . . . unless, of course, it's whispering.

5. Avoid nervous tics and habitual fiddles. I struggle with this issue constantly. I have a tendency—and yes, I know it's bad—when I'm talking to tear up thin strips of paper and crumple them into balls. Not only is this distracting, it demonstrates a lack of concentration on the subject at hand.

6. Don't pace while you're talking—again, another easy habit to fall into. Pacing denotes nervousness, and nervousness represents a lack of confidence.

7. When speaking, remember that pauses without any words are always better than filling in with "ums" and "ers." To *er* may be human, but try to avoid it. It sounds as if you aren't sure of what you're talking about, and we both know that's not the case. Right?

8. The same thing applies to habits such as picking up and restacking PowerPoint slides, opening and closing your briefcase, and clicking your ball-point pen. Any repetitive motion takes away from what you're saying.

9. As my old violin teacher used to say, "If you're going to make a mistake, at least sound like you meant it!" If you find that you've left out something, don't go back and try to stick it in artificially. Whatever you do, don't say, "Oh, I forgot to mention this." That's disorganized and will destroy the client's confidence that you know what you're doing. If you can't organize a simple presentation, how can your company possibly be expected to provide an efficient and reliable service?

10. Be interactive with the client. This is a sales presentation, not a lecture. You want the client to be involved in it, to respond to it, to be excited by it. Remember that earlier in this book I talked about the importance of active listening. There's also such a thing as active talking. It means you frame your presentation in such a way that you constantly elicit comments or questions from the client.

Of course, these are guidelines not just for the first 20 or 30 seconds of your presentation but for the whole thing and into the discussion afterward. But I stress again how important they are to hit at the very beginning. That's when you'll make the biggest impression, and that's when you've got the greatest opportunity to build your client's confidence.

You may be wondering, incidentally, what the result was of that first sales call I made. The answer is . . . I got the sale. It was a bit of a struggle, but I got it. And the fact that I got it improved my confidence, and with it the confidence of the client and many future clients. That's the thought I'd like you to leave this chapter with: the more you do this job—and the more you do it *right*—the more confident you'll become, and in consequence the better you'll get.

CLIENT CHALLENGE: "WHAT'S THIS GOING TO COST ME?"

26

A while back I decided that we needed a new television for the bedroom.

I should make clear that I'm not one of these people who want to have a television in every room of the house. But when we're lying in bed in the evening, it's nice to be able to tune into something—a late-night talk show, a movie, something on the Travel Channel—and doze off to it.

I went to a well-known electronics retailer and started looking through the store's selection of televisions. A salesperson came up to me and asked if he could help.

"I want a TV," I said.

"Well," he replied, gesturing at the banks of screens surrounding us, all playing some football game, "you've come to the right place." He looked around. "This one is on sale right now. Only $1,800."

"No," I said. "That's much more than I want to pay. What have you got for less?"

He led the way to another, smaller television. "This is $1,100."

"Haven't you got anything a bit cheaper?" I said.

He looked at me, thinking, clearly, that I was going to tell him that when I was a boy television sets cost $30 and only the richest families in our little town of Mayberry, USA, could afford one. "Well," he said, "I can sell you this floor model for $700."

I wound up buying that one and took it home, thinking over the experience. It had left a bad taste in my mouth, but I wasn't quite sure why. A while later I was talking to a friend of mine about it while we sat in my living room, sipping drinks.

"How much did you pay for this television?" my friend asked, pointing toward the set in a corner of the room.

I cast my mind back. "$1,900."

"So why," he said, "were you willing to pay more for a set that's out here than for a TV in your bedroom?"

"Because I spend more time watching TV out here," I answered instantly. "The TV experience out here is more important to me." Then I got where he was going with this.

The point is that what's an acceptable price for something—whether it's a physical product like a television or a less tangible one such as a service—is determined not by the product's features but by the value you as a customer attach to it. I was willing to pay more money for a television in the living room because that's where I do the bulk of my TV watching. The set for the bedroom was less important—really just a sleep aid in some respects—so I didn't want to pay much for it.

The lesson for salespeople from this is that one of the first things to find out in a sales call is what value your potential customer attaches to what you're selling. That will determine how you sell and what price you can reasonably sell at.

This is pretty basic—Economics 101, in fact. Demand determines price. (Supply also factors into this, but it's a little deceptive to say, as some people do, that supply determines price. If no one wants a product, the amount of it in circulation doesn't matter. You won't be able to sell it at any price.)

DISCOUNTING SHOULD NOT BE YOUR FIRST OPTION

Price comes up in every sale, but salespeople often struggle with how to handle it. Elsewhere (most recently in *The 25 Toughest Sales Objections*) I've dealt with the tendency of too many salespeople to discount as a kind of default position. Whenever they run into the slightest resistance on price, and sometimes when they run into no resistance at all, they start discounting. This is a serious mistake, not only because it essentially gives away money for little or no reason but because it doesn't start from the important base question: how much does the customer want and need what you're selling? It only makes sense to consider discounts after you know the answer to that question. Even then, as I point out, discounting is a tactic that needs to be used carefully.

Let's see what happens when Larry, a salesperson selling knife-sharpening services to Darina, a grocery-store owner, forgets some of these basic lessons about discounting and finding out what the customer wants.

Larry: And we'll come in once a month to sharpen all the knives that you use on your meat counter. Once every four months we'll come in and do a free knife sharpening for your customers, which will help draw people into the store.

Darina: I see. So, bottom line, how much is this going to cost me?

Larry: Our base package is $400 per month.

Darina: I see.

Larry: However, since you're a first-time customer, for the first six months of the contract we could go down to $350 per month.

Darina: I see. That would be nice.

Larry: In fact, I could take this down to $300 for the first two months if we can come to an agreement today.

Darina: Yes, I think we can do that. Could you increase the free knife-sharpenings to every three months?

Larry: Yes, that wouldn't be a problem. Here's our standard contract; I'll just make the alterations in it right now.

Well, what's the problem? Larry got the sale. And that's the whole point of a sales call, isn't it?

Yes, but only up to a point. Larry got the sale, true, and he'll probably go back to his office pretty happy. But he also discounted twice (really three times, since he increased the number of times per year his company will offer free knife sharpening from three to four). And he didn't need to—he discounted on the price of the package without Darina even asking him to do it. All she did was say, "I see," and sit there.

THE SOUND OF SILENCE

Darina, unlike Larry, understands the power of silence in negotiation. We all have a natural tendency to fill silence. Nature abhors a vacuum, and apparently humans abhor a pause in conversation. Larry interpreted her silence as resistance and caved immediately. So while he got the sale, he also sent a message that he can be pushed around and that he instinctively discounts. You can bet that Darina has stored that information for reference the next time she and Larry talk about anything.

When a prospect asks, "How much is this going to cost me?" what should really kick into your brain is, "How much do you need this?" In other words, what's a fair price that you're going to pay for me to perform this service for you?

I don't want you to come away from this chapter thinking that I object in principle to discounting. I don't. I just think too many salespeople see it as a strategy rather than a tactic and revert to it far too easily. My rule of thumb regarding discounting is this: any discount on one part of a deal should be accompanied by a concession from the prospect on another part of the deal. It's simple— you've got to give in order to get, but when you get, you should be willing to give. This is why negotiation over a sale is to a large extent a matter of determining the exchange of concessions.

With all of this in mind, here's how the conversation might have gone.

Larry: And we'll come in once a month to sharpen all the knives that you use on your meat counter. Once every four months we'll come in and do a free knife sharpening for your customers, which will help draw people into the store.

Darina: I see. So, bottom line, how much is this going to cost me?

Larry: Our base package is $400 per month.

Darina: I see.

Larry: Do you have questions about the price?

Darina: It seems as if it's pushing against the upper limits of our budget.

Larry: I see.

Darina: But on the other hand, I think this service could be of real value to us.

Larry: Yes, we see it in other cases, where people come in to have their knives professionally sharpened. Then it becomes a habit, and before you know it you've increased your regular customer base by offering this free service.

Darina: The question is, is that worth $400 a month. I'm not sure it is.

Larry: Well, we can calculate that if the free sharpening event winds up drawing in five new customers a month, which is a pretty small number, you're looking at five customers who spend, on average, $100 per week on groceries—that's the average family's grocery bill. So that means per month you're looking at increasing your revenues by $2,000. Surely that's a good return on a $400 investment?

Darina: Yes, but I'm concerned about the here and now before those new customers have come in. Can you give me any sort of discount?

Larry: Well, I can extend a new customer discount to you of $350 a month for the first six months of the deal. But to do that, I'd need you to sign a two-year agreement.

Darina: I'm okay with that.

Larry: Great. Let's look at the contract together.

Now that's more like it! Larry's got the sale at a better price than he did the first time, as well as a two-year contract. Darina's got some facts and figures to make her feel more comfortable. And Larry didn't instinctively discount; instead, he turned the silence around on Darina by asking her to fill it with an answer to his question. This is salesmanship at its best.

Remember as well that you've got a lot of things besides price to bargain with. Larry, for instance, had the length of the contract to use as a negotiating point. He might also have negotiated over the number of times his company would offer the knife sharpening for the public, how often they'd sharpen the knives of the meat department, or whether they'd extend their service to sharpening the blades on the electric slicers in the deli section of the store. In any sale there are all kinds of things besides price to discuss. So don't let yourself get boxed in over price. Remember: discounting is a tactic. Use it wisely.

NEGOTIATING
THE AGREEMENT

27

Sales, as I've said in other books, is really all about negotiating. In fact, I'll go further and say that life, in general, is about negotiating. We live on a planet inhabited by billions of people who all want different things, have different expectations, and struggle to achieve different ends. When you think about it, it's rather miraculous that the human race has survived as long as it has.

The reason we have is because we've learned to compromise. We don't, in the immortal words of Mick Jagger, always get what we want. But by trying, we generally get what we need.

Negotiating the agreement to provide a service isn't that different, really, from negotiating any other agreement. Here we'll review some of the basics but add a few more twists. The most important thing to remember is that when you negotiate to provide a service, you're defining something that will be provided over time into the future. That means that the contract has to take some extra things into account.

THE BASICS OF NEGOTIATING SERVICES

The basics of negotiating are pretty simple:

1. Negotiating in a sales situation means you're aiming for a

win-win. If you lose sight of this, you've lost sight of the basic point of the sale. A winning solution is one that works for both the parties, not just one of them.

2. Always allow for some wiggle room. That means never starting as high as you're willing to go or as low as you can possibly accept. Instead, begin in the middle and work outward.

3. Know your walkaway point. Have a clear idea of what's the point at which the sale is no longer worth negotiating.

4. Understand your alternative to making the sale. There are various terms for this among salespeople. One of the most popular is *BATNA* (best alternative to a negotiated agreement). I prefer the term *alternative*. Simply put, this means understanding the cost to you if you don't make the sale versus the cost of making the sale on unfavorable terms.

5. Remember that sooner or later any unresolved issues in the sale are going to be pushed into the open air where everyone can see them. This is one of the biggest reasons why some negotiations lead to sales blowing up—because salespeople try to gloss over or ignore significant differences between them and their clients. Contracts have a way of focusing everyone's minds onto those disagreements, sometimes making them seem more important than they really are.

Each of these five elements will be present in any negotiation. But for services, I want to stress this last one. A service is a long-term relationship with a client. When you sell a product, it's quite possible that this is the one and only time you and the client will be in the same room. The client will use your product and like it or not like it. But you won't have to talk to each other again.

For that reason, product salespeople sometimes take negotiations and their final phase—the contract—less seriously. I think that's a mistake, but I'll talk about that in a different book. For purposes of the conversation that we're having right now, I want to stress that selling a service is different. Instead of a one-time thing, it's a commitment; you and the client are going to be working together for a while. And while it's faintly possible that in selling a product to a client you might be able to gloss over some things at the contract stage, I absolutely guarantee that this won't be the case if you're selling a service.

Fifteen or so years ago I found this out the hard way. I'd negotiated a contract with a client to provide sales training for his people, with a fee based on a percentage of the increase in his sales. But the contract didn't specify, and I didn't ask, if the rate we'd agreed upon was gross or net. In retrospect it seems like a really stupid mistake to make, and I don't know what I was thinking at the time. But the contract didn't explain the point, and I, mistakenly, didn't point this out at the time we signed. We agreed on a five-year term for the contract. But the first time a check showed up from his office in my mailbox I hit the roof.

"What the hell do you mean?" I shouted into the phone. "We agreed on a gross rate!"

"No, we didn't," he snarled back. "Net! We said net!"

"Well, what does the contract say?"

There were a frantic few minutes when we both scrolled through the contract on our screens. Then there was a painful silence when we realized that the contract we'd both signed didn't specify which term applied.

"Well," he said grimly, "we're just going to have to talk about this."

And with a sinking feeling in my stomach, I realized this was a person I was bound to by the terms of the contract for the next five years. They were, I can tell you now, a painful five years, most of them spent wrangling over this and that, and both of us were glad to see the end of them.

That experience sensitized me to this issue. I don't believe that anyone in a sales negotiation goes looking for a fight. But what this episode showed me was how easy it is to get into an antagonistic relationship because one or both of you didn't bother to clarify details in the first place.

Negotiations should be for the long haul. I think that's true of sales negotiations when they involve a physical product, but it's even truer when they involve a service that your company is providing. You need to look to the future.

SERVICES NEGOTIATIONS SHOULD BE WIN-WIN

It's also important to stress the first element of negotiation here: sales is about winning, but it's about winning for both parties, not just you. I can illustrate this with the sad case of my friend Dan.

Dan's company was a very aggressive sales firm. There was tremendous pressure by management for the sales force to perform, to hit their weekly quotas, and to bring in the numbers of sales needed for management to look good to the board. Dan found, he told me later, that he was getting ulcers from the constant pressure. Rather than back off and find a job that didn't require him to check his soul at the door, Dan stayed with the corporation because the pay and benefits were good and the commissions were fantastic. All of this changed (that is, it began to change) when Dan went on a sales call to the ABC Company. He was selling a tax package provided by his company, and management had stressed in their last meeting with the sales force how important it was for everyone to push the service. Dan went into his sales presentation to the ABC Company with both guns blazing. When ABC Company representatives resisted his terms, he pushed them hard, then harder. They wavered, and Dan knew he had them. His macho-ness was reinforced by his image of the white-hatted gunslinger riding into town, vanquishing the bad guys, and then going off into the sunset.

To great accolades Dan returned to his company, contract in hand. He'd forced the management at ABC Company to take the tax package for the next five years. Moreover, he was confident that based on this he could get the LMN Corporation, one of ABC's rivals, to sign onto the program as well, significantly increasing X Corporation's penetration of this corporate sector.

All that went by the wayside, though, when Dan looked at the front page of the *Wall Street Journal* and discovered that the ABC Corporation had just gone bankrupt. Even though, reading the story, he knew that far more was involved than the tax package he had sold the company, he was wracked with guilt. He couldn't eat or sleep, knowing that he'd pressured the company into doing something that, while it might not have actively hurt it, certainly hadn't helped. "I felt like the guy who steered the *Titanic* into the iceberg," he told me later over a dry martini in a Manhattan bar. "I didn't exactly sink the ship—there were lots of other people involved. But I didn't exactly help either."

Dan had been so focused on his own corporation's goals and his own commission that he'd completely ignored the question of what sort of deal would be favorable to his client. I don't, of course, recommend signing agreements that give away the farm to your clients. But surely there's a middle ground. Surely we can recognize when we've gotten to a point that we're both gaining something from the agreement.

Dan, disillusioned with sales, dropped out of the rat race and, the last I heard, was living in upstate Vermont raising cabbages. I'm sure he finds that more peaceful than dealing with the wolves of Wall Street, but you can't walk away from there forever.

What could Dan have done differently in that situation?

Well, broadly speaking, my advice to him would have been to find a different employer, one not as focused on selling at any cost.

I also would have told him that in the long run his best bet was to be completely honest with his client. It isn't as if no one's going to find out the truth about what you've sold. If you're selling a service that has significant defects, this is going to be realized in its performance.

I don't approve of dishonesty in sales—not just for moral reasons, although they're strong, but because from a purely practical point of view that it doesn't work. No one trusts a dishonest salesperson. And there's no place where this becomes more obvious than in the final negotiation about the details of the agreement.

WATCH OUT FOR ICEBERGS!

Negotiating a contract is a little bit like finding your way through a sea filled with icebergs—harking back to our *Titanic* analogy. There are a lot of ways to make a mistake, but if you succeed, you'll find clear sailing ahead. The key to a successful negotiation is to anticipate difficulties, much as the captain of the *Titanic* should have known that there was a significant danger from icebergs. In this spirit, here are some pointers:

1. Like an iceberg, a challenge in a negotiation can have a lot of hidden mass that you can't see. So don't dismiss it easily, but explore it and find out what's involved in it. That way, you won't casually steer over what looks like clear water and find that you've run aground.

2. Always be prepared for emergencies. The *Titanic* disaster was multiplied by the fact that the ship had too few lifeboats for its passengers. You, being a wise negotiator, should anticipate difficulties and be ready for them with prepared answers.

3. Don't be afraid to call for assistance. If you think that you need some help in negotiating the complicated waters of a

deal, talk to other people in your organization. The *Titanic* sent up signal flares when it was in distress, but only when it was too late. Don't make the same mistake.

4. Be prepared to build a better ship if the one you've got sinks. If the service you are offering doesn't work for the client, go back to your organization and figure out what would work. Be innovative. Look for new solutions. Be prepared to think outside the box. In fact, I'd advocate on occasion throwing the box away completely and finding a different paradigm.

Negotiations run throughout the course of a sales call. When negotiating about services, always remember that you're negotiating about a promise of future delivery. The more straightforward you are, the better your chance of coming out on top of things in the end.

CLIENT CHALLENGE: "WHAT GUARANTEES CAN YOU GIVE ME?"

28

All right, I'll say it for the last time: Selling a service is about making promises. You're selling your company's ability to do something, usually better than your client could do it for her- or himself. You're making a promise that the client will realize specific benefits from this service at some point in the future. If you've been listening to me through this book you know that you have to, as much as possible, quantify these benefits in dollars and cents, since ultimately any business exists to make money.

This means that when the rubber hits the road, your service has to do what it says it's going to do. This also means you've got to be precise and straightforward in spelling out just what you're promising.

To a large extent in sales, this is the job of the contract. It's also a part of the pitch and the negotiation, because if you pitch something that you can't really come through on, it's going to make you look dishonest and no one will do business with you. And it's part of the negotiation for the same reason. If, to try to gain an advantage, you promise what you can't deliver, you may win the sale but you'll set up a short relationship and quite possibly a lawsuit against your company. None of these are good outcomes.

But it's in the contract where these issues really come to the fore. When you're writing the contract, you're spelling out the exact terms of the deal and the consequences if either side violates those terms.

Contract language is often written by lawyers. I have a lot of respect for a lot of lawyers, and I understand, after many years, why they tend to try to spell everything out. It's because a lawyer's worst enemy is ambiguity. Ambiguity leads to confusion, lawsuits, and general unhappiness. So lawyers will go out of their way to cross every *t* and dot every *i*. They'll say that the terms of the contract apply "throughout the universe," just on the off chance that we someday travel to the stars and someone on Alpha Centauri wants to enforce the terms of the contract they've written. (I'm not kidding about that, by the way. Take a look at some contracts and see.)

PROBLEMS IN NEGOTIATING GUARANTEES

With all this in mind, we approach the question of guarantees. The client for whom you're performing the service wants iron-clad guarantees of everything. Your legal staff, with an eye toward a future in which anything can and does happen, wants to hedge their language, provide for every conceivable contingency, and be as cautious as possible about guaranteeing anything.

How do you get these two sides to meet?

Let's start by looking at a case in which they don't meet and in fact end up even farther apart. Lisa is a salesperson for a tech services firm, selling to Marie, who's the marketing officer for a small publisher.

Marie: One thing that's very important to us is to set up and maintain a website.

Lisa: Absolutely. That's great for a business of your size that's trying to save a lot of money in traditional marketing costs. A website can be a great way to do social network marketing. We can set up and maintain the site for you.

Marie: When would the site be able to go live?

Lisa: Well, obviously there are a lot of factors to take into consideration here. We'll have to see exactly what your requirements are and then estimate, based on that, when we can launch a beta version of the site for debugging.

Marie: Yes, I understand all that. But we've got a lot of important campaigns coming up in the fall for titles, and I just want a general idea of when the site could be expected to go live.

Lisa: I'd really hate to give you that estimate without some further research.

Marie: Well, this is a problem because without a firm guarantee that the site will go live by June, I don't see that it would be much use for our immediate problem. That's when our fall PR campaigns will launch, and if the site's not functioning by then, we miss that window of opportunity.

Lisa: Sure, I understand, but I don't want to promise something we can't deliver.

Marie: Okay, could the site have forums so that our customers can write in and give their opinions of our titles and have discussions among themselves about them?

Lisa: That's something of a concern, since forums are pretty complicated. You'll need a moderator.

Marie: Can you supply that?

Lisa: Well, I'd hate to commit to that and then have to say no. Why don't we put that down for discussion at our next meeting?

Marie: No, I don't think we need to bother with that because there's not going to be a next meeting. We're all done.

Wow! Lisa had a great opportunity, and she completely blew it. Marie won't do business with her company again, and word will probably spread quickly in the publishing community about how indecisive and commitment shy Lisa's company is. Once that sort of thing gets started, it's really hard to turn around. Wasn't it Mark Twain who said, "A lie can travel halfway round the world while the truth is putting on its shoes"? Except that in this case it's not a lie—Lisa really is wishy-washy.

This is a good example of a salesperson who's scared to give a guarantee because she's afraid she may get her company in trouble. As I've said elsewhere, I'm a strong proponent of making sure you don't make big promises without checking with your front office, but the problem here is that Lisa sounds as if she doesn't want to commit. She gives the impression (probably rightly) that she's more concerned with protecting her company than with helping Marie's company solve its problem.

GUIDELINES FOR NEGOTIATING GUARANTEES

Here are some guidelines for negotiation on guarantees:

1. **Don't overcommit.** Don't make promises that you're sure your company won't be able to keep. Lisa doesn't want to bind her company to promising a live website by June, but it would be equally wrong for her to commit to getting one up two weeks from now.

2. **Don't undercommit.** This, of course, is the particular sin of which Lisa is guilty, and it's just cost her the sale.

3. **Make layered guarantees.** This is really the secret to solving the problem. An absolute guarantee is a problem ("I'll absolutely promise that we'll have your website up and running in three months' time") because the future

contains all sorts of imponderables. You could have a fire at your facility. You could run into challenges in creating the website in the first place, let alone getting it functioning and tested. We could have a mad hedgehog invasion. Who knows? But you can sort those contingencies into possible (challenges to creating the site); less possible (a fire or some other significant disaster at your company); and highly improbable (mad hedgehog invasion—although stranger things have happened). Your guarantee can be phrased along the lines of "We believe we can have your site constructed, tested, and live in three months' time, provided we don't run into any big issues along the way."

When it comes time to write the contract, your legal team can incorporate the various layers of these guarantees into the document so that your company is fully protected while at the same time fully committed to providing the service you've sold.

Part of the art of guarantees is to be up-front in discussing them and their various layers with the client. You have to be careful not to qualify them to death, and you want to always keep the tone of the discussion positive. But you can also make it very clear that, as Ben Franklin said, the only two sure things in this world are death and taxes.

Now let's consider this conversation as it might have happened if Lisa had focused on selling instead of backpedaling and on layered guarantees instead of shying like a frightened horse at the very thought of a guarantee.

Marie: One thing that's very important to us is to set up and maintain a website.

Lisa: Absolutely. That's great for a business of your size that's trying to save a lot of money in traditional marketing costs. A website can be a great way to do social network marketing. We can set up and maintain the site for you.

Marie: When would the site be able to go live?

Lisa: Our general experience in doing this for other companies is that from the time we sign the contract to the time the site goes live takes four months.

Marie: Hm. That's a problem because a lot of our fall promotions begin in June, and we want to have a functioning website to use by then.

Lisa: Obviously I can't make an absolute commitment to having the site go live in June because there are all sorts of contingencies we'll have to take into account. But I think if we can sign the contract this week, we can put this on accelerated development by our team and aim for a launch date of June 20. Would that work for you?

Marie: Yes. We could work with that.

Lisa: Because this is on such a tight deadline, what I'd like to write into the contract is a series of milestones during the three months of development. That way we can check that we're on track, and if we get off track at least we'll know by how much and have an idea of what we need to do to fix it.

Marie: I agree. That seems very sensible. I wanted to ask about forums on the site, so that our customers can comment on our titles and have conversations among themselves.

Lisa: Would you be administering these forums, or would you want us to do it?

Marie: You would have to do it; we don't have the staff to handle it.

Lisa: This is a bit tricky only because moderating a forum can take quite a lot of time, especially if, as we hope, the forum becomes very lively and involves a lot of people. I think we should make this a "stretch goal" in the contract for June. If we can get forums up and running by June along with the rest of the site, we'll be paid a small bonus one-time fee; if not, then we'll commit to having the forums up within two months of the site's launch.

Marie: Yes, I think that will work. I'll have to check with my boss, of course.

Lisa: Yes, I'll have to clear all this with my boss and with our legal team as well. Suppose we get together again next week at 10 a.m. on Tuesday?

Marie: Fine.

Now we're getting somewhere. Lisa hasn't made an impossible commitment of time and resources to achieving the goal of a June website. Instead, she's suggested an intermittent step: the milestones, written into the contract so both sides agree on them. This is great because it gives both Lisa and Marie a way of evaluating the guarantee and making sure it's working.

On the forums, Lisa's actually negotiated an incentive for her company to do this on time. The one-time bonus will be something she can bring back to her bosses to persuade them to approve the deal. And Marie's gotten what she wants: a reasonable hope that she'll have a functioning website with forums in the timeframe she needs it. As in all good sales, the situation's a win-win.

THE IMPORTANCE OF CUSTOMER SERVICE

29

Everyone has bad customer service stories; there are whole websites devoted to tales of customer service horror (to be fair, there are also websites that give examples of completely unreasonable or stupid customers, but that's another problem). I'll give you one example from my own recent experience.

Several years ago I purchased a portable DVD player for my wife. She travels quite a bit, and I thought it would be nice for her, while she was on the train, to be able to watch her favorite movies or television shows. She was delighted with the player and made very good use of it.

Then, close to a year after I purchased it, something went wrong and the player stopped working. I made some disparaging comments about the quality of workmanship that had obviously gone into it and took it back to the large electronics store where I'd bought it. I was directed to the customer service desk, and a polite young man asked me some questions about the player and what was wrong with it.

So far, so good.

He informed me that the manufacturer's warranty was still good on the device and told me they'd give me a call when it was ready.

Several weeks went by. Then several more. Then another. I called the store and asked to speak to the service department. "Where's my DVD player?" I asked. "I didn't think it would take five weeks to fix it."

"Oh," answered the voice at the other end of the phone, "we didn't fix it ourselves. Because the manufacturer warranty was still good, we sent it back to them for repair."

"I see," I said, wondering in the back of my mind why they couldn't have told me that in the first place. "When do they say it's going to be ready?"

"Well," he said airily, without even a note of concern in his voice, "we don't know because they never return our phone calls or e-mails. I guess it'll be ready when it's ready."

I took a deep breath. "Do you mean," I asked, my voice barely under control, "that you sent this gadget to be repaired and you're not even in touch with the people doing the repair?"

He mumbled something, and I asked to speak to a manager. From her I got the same story. "This is outrageous!" I told her. "What happens if they've lost it? What if it takes them six months ... or a year ... or 10 years to send it back? What do you do then?"

I could feel her shrugging as she answered, "You're just going to have to live with it."

The happy ending to this story is that, possibly as a result of my phone call, within a week we got the repaired DVD player back. The unhappy ending, from the store's point of view, is that I will never shop there again, and I've told my story to as many of my friends as were interested.

BAD CUSTOMER SERVICE HAS FAR-REACHING EFFECTS

Bad customer service is like throwing a rock into a pool of water; you can see the ripples spreading outward. In today's age of the Internet, when all sorts of sites exist to communicate customer complaints and anecdotes, you can be sure that if you give bad service to one person, dozens—maybe hundreds or thousands—will hear about it.

In my case, of course, what was involved was a physical product, but there was also a service aspect to the matter. In the case of a company that sells nothing but a service, bad customer reviews can be devastating. After all, if people don't like one of your products, there's at least a reasonable chance that they might buy others. But if people don't like the service you provide, they'll go elsewhere and tell all their friends and acquaintances about the bad experience you gave them.

This is why one of the points I emphasize when talking to salespeople who are in the business of selling services is the importance of customer service. There are two parts to this. First, you have to demonstrate to the client that the service you're selling has a strong customer service aspect—if, for instance, you're selling a PR consulting service and there's a serious error, such as a missed PR opportunity or a badly communicated PR message, the client will want to know how your company plans to fix the problem in the quickest and most efficient way.

Second—and this is an important one—if you, the salesperson, make a mistake during the course of negotiations, you have to be ready to fix it immediately without fuss and feathers. Such a mistake may be completely unrelated to the type of service you're trying to sell. Nonetheless, the client sees your ability to fix the problem as a forerunner of how your service will perform. Correctly, he or she sees you as an indication of how seriously your company takes its customers.

THE HIGHEST PRIORITY

Consider, for instance, the following situation:

You're in the middle of negotiations with four different clients.

It's a short week because of a holiday coming up, and you're trying to wrap everything up as quickly as possible. On top of that, your child is sick at home, and your in-laws are coming for a visit, which means you're going to have to leave work early and go home to help your spouse clean the house. Suddenly, as you're collecting your things preparatory to leaving the office, the phone rings.

"Damn!" you think as you pick it up. "Who is it this time?"

It's one of your four prospects, and he's hopping mad. "Steve," he shouts, "you were supposed to call me this morning at 10 a.m. sharp. I moved around three appointments to make time for you, and you never called. What's going on?"

A lot of things are running through your mind: you're tired and grumpy, this guy isn't by any means the biggest or most important of the prospects you're working with right now, the reason you forgot the 10 a.m. call was because you were composing an important e-mail to a much bigger customer, and if you don't wrap up this phone call in about three minutes you'll miss your train and your spouse will kill you when you get home.

There are three choices here (well, more than three, actually, but let's keep things simple):

1. You can blow the prospect off and get out of the office. Sure, you'll lose the sale, but at this point who cares? You're pretty sure you're going to be able to sign the other three prospects, and that'll still leave you with a nice commission, not to mention some kudos from the front office. You'll make your train, and the weekend will probably run relatively smoothly.

2. You can say, "Gee, I'm sorry. I'm on my way out the door right now, but let's touch base on Monday after the holiday" and hang up the phone before he's got a chance to go any further. He'll be mad over the weekend, but you can

always pick up the pieces next week. It'll probably all work out for the best. And right now the last thing you feel like doing is dealing with an angry voice at the other end of the telephone.

3. You can put down your briefcase, take off your coat, sit down at your desk, and deal with the problem. You'll definitely miss your train and probably have an unpleasant conversation when you get home (although you hope your spouse will understand when you explain what happened). But the most important thing is that you'll keep the prospect calm and salvage the situation.

The correct answer, of course, is number 3. Here's why:

- The fact that the prospect's account is a relatively small one is entirely irrelevant. You strive, as a good salesperson, to treat all clients equally. Of course you're conscious that some accounts are much bigger than others and will, inevitably, take up more of your time. But a dissatisfied customer, even a small one, can do a lot of damage, just as a big one can.

- Putting off fixing a problem just makes the prospect angrier. It's a sign of disrespect, a statement that "Whatever I did to get you mad at me is less important than what I'm doing right now." That's never a good message to send.

- The customer, or in this case, the prospect, always comes first. That's a golden rule of selling.

Notice that the problem here has nothing to do with whatever service you're selling to the prospects. But the fact that you missed an important phone call is telling the prospect that as a salesperson you're unreliable. And if that's the case with you, it's probably true of your company.

Selling a service means you're selling a promise. Anything you do at any point in the sale to undermine that promise makes it less likely you'll successfully complete the sale.

A further point to make in this regard is that customer service isn't just a reactive proposition. Too many companies seem to think that once they've sold you something, the next time they should have any contact with you is when you want to buy something else. I think that's nonsense.

Look at this in light of a very common experience, one that you're very likely to have encountered at one time or another. Recently while on a sales call, I stopped by a restaurant for a quick bite to eat. The host seated me right away, the server showed up promptly and took my order. The food was at the table quickly—a good thing since I didn't have very much time.

But then something happened that wasn't so good. I didn't see the server again until I was done with the meal. As I was refolding my napkin, he sauntered up to the table and asked, "All done?"

"Yes."

"Was everything okay?"

I was irritated, and it probably showed. "As a matter of fact," I said, "my hamburger was overdone. I asked for it medium rare and it came well done."

He looked blank. "Oh," he said. "You want me to bring you another one?"

I couldn't believe it. I'm not as thin as I once was, but I can't put away two hamburgers at lunch. Besides, I had to get back on the road. "No," I said, "just the check."

This sort of thing is played out hundreds of times across the country every day, and it's indicative of how little restaurants teach servers about good service. The server should have done two things. First, when he brought the food he should have lingered for a moment to make sure I had everything I wanted and that the food was satisfactory. Second, he should have checked back a few minutes later and asked, "Is everything okay?" Those two little things, taking perhaps a total of 30 seconds to a minute, would have made the difference between bad service and good. They also would have ensured that he got a tip; I left him nothing.

The waiter was selling service—an important distinction from the restaurant, which was selling food. He failed in his mission because he was reactive rather than proactive. In the same way, you can ensure a great customer experience by following up with your clients after you've made a sale to make sure everything's okay and that they don't have any complaints about what you've sold them or how you sold it to them. Don't wait for them to call you with a problem. Even if you struggled to make the sale and finished it with a vast sense of relief (a feeling I've had many times when dealing with problem clients), remember: you've got to keep talking to these people. That's how long-term sales relationships are built, and that's how you'll keep on selling.

CONCLUSION

In the trial scene of Lewis Carroll's *Alice's Adventures in Wonderland*, the White Rabbit reports the finding of some verses that may have a bearing on the case of the Knave who stole the tarts.

"Read them," said the King.

The White Rabbit put on his spectacles. "Where shall I begin, please your Majesty?" he asked.

"Begin at the beginning," the King said, very gravely, "and go on till you come to the end: then stop."

There's some good advice for authors there. As any writer will tell you, the hardest part of writing a book is beginning it; the second hardest part is stopping.

This seems like a good place to stop. We've talked extensively about the difference between selling a product and selling a service, and we've reviewed a lot of the basics of selling and established a few new ones. Now I'm going to tell you a last secret: *A service is a product.*

That's right—you heard me. A service is a kind of product. It's just that it's one without a physical manifestation in the here and now. Rather, it's a promise of future actions on your part and future benefits for your client. That's why the fundamentals of selling don't really change whether what you're selling is a physical product or a service. Really, it's just the emphasis that's different.

I've spent some time now traveling around the country and around the world, speaking to different groups of salespeople and other gatherings. I've talked to thousands of people, both in huge halls and in conference rooms and offices. Many of my best conversations have been one-on-one with individuals who were willing to tell me their experiences selling and their thoughts about the way in which the profession is changing.

Based on that, I can tell you that the most important thing for you to be aware of and to integrate into all of your selling today is this: everything's changed.

Some of the change, of course, is the result of the growth of the Internet. Even 15 or 20 years ago it was pretty obvious to anyone paying attention that this phenomenon was going to create a huge change in the way humans communicated. One thing I don't believe was anticipated at the time was the extent to which the Internet increased the sheer volume of information that's widely available. This has become a problem because more information on a topic doesn't necessarily mean more enlightenment. Not all information is equal, and the amount of misinformation, distortion, and just plain nonsense that's peddled online these days is truly frightening.

A second thing that's changed in conjunction with this is the nature of your customers. They've got their own sources of information these days, and they don't need to rely on you to espouse the benefits of what you're selling. Instead, they can go online to customer chat rooms and forums and exchange experiences and opinions. That's good if you're confident in the service you're providing, and plenty of salespeople have made a huge splash using social media to spread the word about their services. But it also means that any mistake you make, any bad experience a customer has with your company, is quickly going to be magnified a thousandfold as it spreads around the world via the Internet.

As a result, you'll often find that customers are both more knowledgeable and more cautious about making a quick commitment.

A third thing that has changed is, well, change itself. When I started selling, change generally came slowly. Now it comes at a fantastic pace. Earlier I mentioned Moore's Law, which says that the number of transistors that can be placed on an integrated circuit doubles approximately every two years. This means that our computing technology is growing at a pace unheard of in human history. It also means that we struggle as a society to keep up with that pace of technological change.

So it's no good assuming that the same old methods of selling will work. You can't walk into your client's office and pull out the same tired old brochures and PowerPoint slides that you've been using for the past 20 years. You can't expect a new prospect to sit all dewy-eyed while you give the same spiel you've been handing out your whole career.

Instead, you've got to be involved in a constant process of self-reinvention and reevaluation. Every time you leave a sales call, you've got to ask yourself, What went well? What could I do better? What didn't the prospect respond to? And how can I grab his or her interest right off the bat?

But—and here's the tricky bit—I *don't* believe this means you should throw the baby out with the bathwater. Yes, you've got to reinvent yourself and how you sell, but at the core of your sales process is the same tried-and-true set of skills and methods you've been using:

Ask questions.

Find out the client's problem.

Help her or him solve the problem.

Put the client first.

And all the other techniques I've been expounding in my books for three and a half decades.

I was speaking to a client in Singapore who is a cross-country cyclist. He told me that when he's riding, he looks far ahead of where he's at; that is to say, he projects himself to the farthest point he can see.

"But," I said, "then how do you navigate the ruts in the road or a hill without looking down?"

He smiled. "By seeing farther ahead," he replied, "my mind can deal with the issues of the road beforehand. So I don't worry about falling off."

Absolutely brilliant! Rather than narrowly focusing on what's directly in front of him, he looks for the problem area before he gets to it. He calculates that into the way he's riding the bike. He doesn't have to look at what's under his feet because he's already seen it—when it was 100 feet away.

I can't think of a better metaphor for good sales—for physical products, but *especially* when you're selling services. You should be seeing problems and questions a long time before they're going to happen, and by doing that, you make the road safe for everyone.

Good selling!

INDEX

0 1341 1464258 7